T0193260

If We Only Knew

IGNORANCE MAY
NOT BE BLISS

WAYNE KNIFFEN

WESTBOW
PRESS®
A DIVISION OF THOMAS NELSON
& ZONDERVAN

WestBow Press books may be ordered through booksellers or by contacting:

WestBow Press
A Division of Thomas Nelson & Zondervan
1663 Liberty Drive
Bloomington, IN 47403
www.westbowpress.com
844-714-3454

Because of the dynamic nature of the Internet, any web addresses or links contained in this book may have changed since publication and may no longer be valid. The views expressed in this work are solely those of the author and do not necessarily reflect the views of the publisher, and the publisher hereby disclaims any responsibility for them.

Any people depicted in stock imagery provided by Getty Images are models, and such images are being used for illustrative purposes only. Certain stock imagery © Getty Images.

Scripture marked (NKJV) taken from the New King James Version®. Copyright © 1982 by Thomas Nelson. Used by permission. All rights reserved.

Scripture quotations marked (NLT) are taken from the Holy Bible, New Living Translation, copyright ©1996, 2004, 2015 by Tyndale House Foundation. Used by permission of Tyndale House Publishers, Carol Stream, Illinois 60188. All rights reserved.

Scripture quotations marked TPT are from The Passion Translation®. Copyright © 2017, 2018, 2020 by Passion & Fire Ministries, Inc. Used by permission. All rights reserved. ThePassionTranslation.com.

ISBN: 978-1-6642-7608-6 (sc)
ISBN: 978-1-6642-7609-3 (hc)
ISBN: 978-1-6642-7607-9 (e)

Library of Congress Control Number: 2022915516

Print information available on the last page.

WestBow Press rev. date: 08/29/2022

To the best elder ever; one of my strongest supporters and encouragers, an incredible spiritual brother, and a faithful friend: Ken Branum.

Contents

Foreword

One of the greatest privileges of my postretirement life was to attend a meeting in Hereford, Texas, every Tuesday morning for eight years with several people from around the panhandle of Texas. Many of us traveled ninety or more round-trip miles each Tuesday to talk about God's grace with special emphasis on the topic of the Great Exchange. (More on that in a moment.) It was a beautiful thing to observe how our joint exploration of God's kingdom could transcend the walls of human-made denominations.

It was during those Tuesday meetings that I met, interacted with, and learned from Wayne Kniffen and other dear friends, all of whom are hungry to deepen their fellowship with the living God and with each other. Even though my wife and I no longer live in Texas, my extensive notes from those meetings continue to be a source of wisdom and inspiration. Those notes contain contributions from all the participants in the meeting, but I believe we all would agree that Wayne was particularly gifted with the ability to express kingdom truths with great clarity. That is why I was so pleased to learn that the wonderful things Wayne had been preaching and teaching for so many years were beginning to come together in the form of books that are now available to a global market.

Since two of Wayne's books have already been published, I would like to take a moment to give you my version of a bird's-eye view of how this third book joins the others as another piece of a puzzle that will continue to reveal the beautiful portrait of God's love and peace. (Yes, Wayne, we look forward to more books in the future!)

In the first half of John 10:10 (NKJV), Jesus said that the enemy of our souls comes with one purpose in mind, and that is to steal, kill, and destroy. In his first book, *The Scam*, Wayne reveals that the primary thing this thief wants to steal from us is our true identity. If we permit that thief to steal our identity, then he has rendered us combat ineffective when it comes to fighting the good fight of faith. The symptoms of this theft include the inevitable spiritual burnout that comes from the self-imposed pressure to "perform" for God and the nagging sense that we never quite succeed; feeling like a spiritual failure and therefore feeling unloved by God; and living a hollow, inauthentic life where we just go through the motions.

In the second half of John 10:10 (NKJV), Jesus contrasted His own mission with that of the thief when He said that He came so that we might have not only life, but abundant life. In his second book, *The Exchange*, Wayne reveals the staggering extent of just how far Jesus was willing to go to deliver that gift of abundant life to us. (See, for example, 2 Corinthians 5:21 and 8:9, NKJV). Wayne unfolds the vast implications of the Great Exchange for our daily lives—implications that have drawn people for decades to that Tuesday meeting in Hereford so that they can "soak" in these truths and then watch their lives being transformed by them.

This third book to emerge from Wayne's overflowing spirit continues to unveil the great feast that has been set before us by our loving Father. This book is not simply a list of facts, theories, or catchy phrases we can use to make ourselves or others feel better. No, this is more of a user's manual that helps us move from simply knowing about the abundant (exchanged) life into actually *living* that life of intimate union with Jesus. It is interesting to observe how many unbelievers can quote the phrase "The truth will make you free," perhaps without realizing that Jesus is the one who said them (John 8:32, NKJV). Wayne follows Jesus's lead by telling the rest of the story. If we examine the context, we find that Jesus said that if we are His disciples, then we shall know the truth. Only then—that is, only after we know the truth—is that truth able to set us free. Now we can understand what the title of this book is designed to tell us. If we only knew these truths, then these truths would be able to set us free. You will notice that each chapter title in this book begins with "If we only knew," followed by the name of the truth that is set forth in the chapter.

Especially in chapters 5 and 6, you will discover that this book is written by a man who has been, and still is, standing tall on the solid rock of Christ even as the enemy of our souls keeps trying to knock him down. From the physical battlefields of Vietnam to the spiritual battles brought about by the sudden death of his firstborn child and their soon-to-be-born baby, to his precious wife's ongoing, years-long fight against cancer, Wayne Kniffen shares with us golden nuggets of truth that have been hard won in some of the deepest and darkest pits life can throw at us. (Only a person like that can write books such as these.) Even in the depths of that darkness, the light of truth has enabled Wayne to chisel out and carry these practical truths from the depths back up to the surface so that we can see and live them.

My prayer for you, dear reader, is a confident one: namely that, as you read these pages, you will be set free as you find rest in the finished work of Jesus and allow truth Himself to do His tender, loving work in your heart.

John O'Brien
Colorado Springs, Colorado

Preface

The Spirit of God was moving in an unprecedented way in our church and in our community. Our church family was buzzing with life. One of our Wednesday night services lasted until almost 11:00 p.m. What made this service even more unusual was that everyone was totally oblivious to the time. Attendance was growing exponentially, people were receiving Christ as their personal Lord and Savior in numbers, the number of first-time visitors were increasing, giving was on the rise—everything a pastor dreams of experiencing in his or her ministry was unfolding.

For over three months, my days were very long. The amazing thing about this is that there was not one time that I got tired. It was an extraordinary season. My mornings started early, and I would work late into the evening. The phone rang constantly. People would call, wanting me to talk to their kids, family members, and neighbors about accepting and receiving Christ as their Lord and Savior. I had the joy and privilege of leading many to Christ over the phone. In one church service alone, we baptized eighty-six adults.

Just before one of our Sunday services started, a young couple stopped me in the hallway for a pleasant good morning chat. This was a great couple. They were heavily involved in the life of our church and were always ready and willing to serve in any area of ministry where there was a need. In our short conversation, they told me how exciting things were and how thrilled they were to be a part of what was going on. What they said next quickened my spirit: "Something is missing, Pastor, and we don't know what it is." My response to them was, "I hear you. Let's keep our eyes on Jesus, stay in bible study, keep witnessing, invite people to church, and give and pray." I gave them the proverbial list of religious activities that we have become so accustomed and addicted to.

They assured me they would continue chasing after God as they made their way into the worship service. I knew in my innermost being that what this couple said was true, because I too felt that something was missing. But just like them, I could not put my finger on what it was. It took me about twenty years to discover what this young couple could not figure out and what I did not have the answer to. I could not give them what I did not have. You cannot impart what you do not know.

What was missing that these two precious people could sense in their spirits but could not identify? They knew something was not being fulfilled. Just like this young couple, I knew something was within our reach, but I did not know what it was. What was it? It was the truth about our identities as believers. It was knowing who we are as new creations in Christ. Yes, it is that simple. The reason something so simple becomes complicated is because it flies in the face of what most of us have been taught about who we are as Christians. Most of what we have been taught about our identities as believers is in lockstep with our experiences, so we assume that what we have been taught must be true. Assumption is the lowest form of knowledge. It has never dawned on most of us that our experiences are not the standard for truth. Most believers never discover who they are as new creations in Christ. As important as most of our faith activities may be, we should do them because we get to, not because we have to. We don't do good things in order to become who we will be in Christ. We do the right things because of who we already are in Christ. Our doing comes out of our beings: we don't do to become. If only we knew.

It is so easy to identify ourselves as sinners saved by grace. Why is this understanding of identity so easy for Christians to embrace? We know we are saved, and we know there are times we sin, so it stands to reason that we are sinners saved by grace. Our experiences support this position. Most of the time, it never registers with us that maybe our experiences may not be the truth. The word of God is truth (John 17:17, NKJV). That means I must never interpret truth based on my experience. I must demand that my experience comes into alignment with the truth. My experiences are always in flux. The truth will always be the truth because it is the truth. Truth is immutable, and truth is unimpeachable.

When Jesus had His encounter with the Samaritan woman at Jacob's well, He did not attack her adultery. He confronted her idolatry. Her spiritual adultery was worse than her physical adultery (John 4:19–24, NKJV). Jesus knew that if she started believing right, she would start living right. Once a person begins to get a revelation about his or her new-creation identity, who Christ has made them to be, it is a new ball game. Do not think for one minute that Jesus approved of this Samaritan woman having five marriages or that He condoned her living with someone who was not her husband. The way Jesus dealt with this woman proves there is something we may not know. It is something that most believers have not discovered yet.

If we say that we believe right but we are behaving wrong, we are living in deception. When we start believing right, especially when it comes to who we are in Christ, we will start behaving right.

If we only knew the gift of God.

If We Only Knew

A Gift Is a Container
with Content

Did you know that it is possible to accept a gift and not receive it? The Greek word for receive (*lambano*) and the Greek word for accept (*dechomai*) are almost synonymous terms, but at times, they can be distinct from one another. It is possible for a person to be given something and not receive it in a favorable way. You can accept a gift and not receive it. Over the years, I have been given gifts that I certainly did not receive. Some of them stayed in their secret place in the closet until they became *rewrapped gifts* that I graciously and cheerfully shared at church life group parties. Don't judge me. I know it does not take a generous heart to give a gift that you have never received.

A person can be given a compliment and not receive it. They may not feel worthy to be complimented. They smile and say thank you, but it never makes its way into their innermost being. The compliment was accepted, but it was not received. The compliment remains unwrapped. I know folks who have been given an apology and say they have accepted it, but then continue to stew over it for years. The apology was accepted, but it was not received. A person can be accepted into a group and never be received by some of the members of that group.

A Gift Is a Wrapped Container That Has Content

We call wrapped packages underneath a Christmas tree gifts. It is fun to watch people as they try to figure out what is inside their packages. Sometimes they will shake the gift to see if the rattle will give them a clue as to what is inside. Gifts are given at other special occasions, like birthdays, anniversaries, or retirement celebrations. A gift is a wrapped container that has content. To receive the content, you must accept the gift. The content of the container is what the gift is all about. A gift can be accepted and the content never enjoyed because it was never opened. A gift must be accepted before the content of the gift is accessible. A gift must be received before the content of the gift is available.

The greatest gift that was ever given was when God gave His Son. "For *God so loved* the world that *He gave His only begotten Son*, that whoever believes in Him should not perish but have everlasting life" (John 3:16, NKJV; emphasis added). The intensity of God's love for us is seen in this verse, "God *so loved* us." What does love do? Love gives.

Paul penned these words in the book of Romans: "For the wages of sin is death, but the gift of God is eternal life in Christ Jesus our Lord" (Romans 6:23, NKJV). The gift that God has given to us is priceless. It is a new life that never ends because it is everlasting. The new life we have been gifted with has no beginning, either, because it is eternal. Jesus is the container, and the quality of life that every soul cries out for is the content of this container.

The reason so many Christians struggle in their faith walk is because they are not enjoying the content of the gift they have been given. They have *accepted* Jesus as their Lord and Savior, but they have not *received* Him. He has been tucked away in a secret place in the closet of their hearts. They are going to heaven, but that does not guarantee they will have a heavenly time getting there. Their life is *just OK*. Just being OK may be a good hook in a commercial slogan, but it is not the abundant life Jesus came to give. What makes life fulfilling is when we begin to discover and appropriate the abundant life that is available only in Christ. It is one thing to read about the birthright benefits we have been given, but it is another thing to enjoy those birthright privileges. We accept Christ, but we do not receive all the wonderful things He came to provide for us. *If we only knew.*

God's present (Jesus) brought His presence into the earth realm (Galatians 4:4, NKJV). Jesus is the wrapped container. He is the gift. In Him is not only life, but a life that is abundant (John 10:10, NKJV). Jesus overflows with content. God loves you so much that He wrapped Himself up in the person of Jesus and gave Himself to you as a gift. Jesus is not just God's present to you Jesus is God's presence in you.

A Picture Is Worth a Thousand Words

They say a picture is worth a thousand words. Let's see if I can paint a picture in your mind. You have been given a beautifully wrapped present. Whoever wrapped it must have been a professional because it is perfect in every way. Everything seemed to be in slow motion as you reached out with both hands to accept it. You are almost in shock that someone would give you such an extravagant gift. Your grip on the gift is firm but gentle. You walk away, pressing the gift lovingly to your chest. You, of all people, have just been given the gift of a lifetime, and you did absolutely nothing to deserve it. When you are eating, sleeping, or just sitting around, the gift is cradled in your arms. The gift is never out of your sight. You are always talking to your friends about the beautiful gift you have been given. Even strangers have heard how you were blessed with this priceless gift. All you can do is shake your head in unbelief as you mumble to yourself, "I cannot believe this is mine."

After several years of loving on your gift, you run in to the person who gave it to you. You were not expecting the question he or she asked you. "Have you enjoyed your gift?" the person asked you. "Did it fit?"

"Fit?" you ask in bewilderment. "What do you mean fit?" Your face begins to pale. The shock that you are feeling now makes it impossible for you to see the person's face. His or her voice sounds like it is oscillating through a tunnel. "I had it made especially for you. There is not another one like it in all the world," the gift-giver says. Then the person asks, "May I see your gift for a moment?"

Reluctantly, you slowly hand them the gift that you accepted from them years ago. You can hear the paper being torn as the gift is being opened. You cannot believe this person has the audacity to unwrap your beautiful gift. Once the container has been opened, you are able to see the contents, and you are speechless. You cannot believe your eyes. "That is mine?" you say. Your breath is taken away by the beauty of what you see inside the package. Words cannot describe its glory. It has been yours all these years, and you did not know it. You had accepted the gift, but you never received it. The contents of the beautiful container were yours the moment you accepted it, but you never enjoyed the gift that was inside the package.

Are you beginning to get the picture? When we accepted Jesus (God's gift to the world) as our Lord and Savior, we not only got Him; we got everything that was in Him as well. There is more in the container than forgiveness for our sins. That, in and of itself, would be worth accepting the gift. But there is more—so much more. Jesus said that He came to give us life, a life that is abundant.

We Can Enjoy the Content of a Gift without Neglecting the Gift Itself

What is the greatest gift that God has ever given to humankind? If this question were asked to a group of serious believers, their answer would probably be unanimous. The greatest gift that God has ever given is His Son, Jesus Christ. That would be the correct answer. But if you pay attention, it will not take long before the answer begins to morph into things like salvation, forgiveness, eternal life, victory, and the list goes on. It does not take long before all the wonderful birthright benefits that become ours at the moment we accept and receive Jesus as our Lord and Savior, begin to overshadow the gift. Without even realizing it, the content becomes the most important thing to us. Thank God for the contents of the gift, but the gift (Jesus) must always be our first love. Why? "For in Him [Jesus] we live and move and have our being" (Acts 17:28, NKJV; emphasis added). Without Jesus Christ, we have no birthright benefits. When we keep things in their proper perspective, then we can enjoy all our birthright benefits and still keep the most important thing, the most important thing—Christ.

We see this truth played out before our very eyes in the story Jesus told about a father who had two sons. In rebellion and rude disrespect for his father, the youngest son left home with the mindset of independence. He did not want to submit to any authority. Doing what he wanted to do, when he wanted to, and how he wanted to do it, was his motivation for leaving his father. Things did not work out so well for this young man. The freedom he thought he was going to find, actually made him a slave. He was a son but living like a servant. The moment came when his options for survival were reduced to two choices. He could continue to live with the pigs and probably die an early death, or he could return to his father. He chose to return to his father. This was the wisest decision he had made in a while. True freedom is found in humble submission.

The reception he got from his father when he returned home was not what he had expected. His father received him unconditionally. There were no strings attached, not even "I told you so." Even though the young man was willing to take the position of a servant in his father's home, his father treated him like a son. The father threw a big party to celebrate his son's return.

The father had his servants place the best robe on his son. A ring was put on his finger, sandals were placed on his feet, and the fatted calf was prepared for the homecoming celebration. In the blink of an eye, this young, rebellious son became the honored guest of a huge celebration. He was given what he did not deserve, birthright privileges. He discovered that his father had more grace in his heart than he had sin in his life. He was born a son. Therefore, he did not lose with his bad works what he did not get with his good works.

There he is, the honored guest. What do you think captured his attention more than anything else? The best robe? Surely, it was something to behold. The robe covered the soiled garments that he had on, as well as his stained, dirty body. Or maybe it was the ring. The ring was actually the family credit card. If anyone did not deserve access to the family treasury, it was this young man. He had already proven he was not trustworthy. The new sandals he was now wearing must have felt good on his bruised and battered feet. I can see him rocking back and forth, listening to the new leather squeak. The smell of the fatted calf that had been prepared must have been intoxicating, an aroma that was so much better than the smell of the pigs he had just left.

Which gift do you think he treasured the most, the robe, the ring, the sandals, or the fatted calf? My answer would be none of them. I do not think he could take his eyes off his father. The greatest gift he had been given was his father. His birthright privileges were nothing short of amazing, but the most important thing in his life was his father. He was able to survive and thrive because of his father.

As I mentioned, the prodigal son would gladly have accepted the position of a servant in his father's house. After all, his father's servants lived a much better life than this son was living at the time. This young man was willing to live like a slave even though he was a son, just like so many children of God today. Many slaves in this world's system are enjoying a better life than many God's sons and daughters, and it is not because we have a stingy and hard-to-please heavenly Father. It is because of our ignorance, our not knowing what is rightfully ours because of our being born from above.

Paid in Full

The story is told of a young man who was about to graduate from college. He had his heart set on a beautiful sports car that was in the showroom of a local dealership for his graduation gift. Knowing that his father could afford the car, he told his father that this was all he wanted for his graduation.

As this special day was approaching, the young man kept looking for signs that his dad had bought the car. On the day he was to graduate, his dad called him into the den. He told him how proud he was to have such a fine son and how much he loved him. Then he handed him a beautifully wrapped gift box.

The young man had disappointment written all over his face, but he was curious as to what was inside the gift. When he got the box open, his disappointment could no longer be controlled. Inside the box was a beautiful leather-bound bible with his name embossed on it. He did not want a bible! He had his heart set on that sports car. In his anger, he raised his voice to his dad. "With all the money you have, you give me a bible. You knew I wanted that car." Then he stormed out of the house, leaving the bible behind.

Many years passed, and the young man became very successful in the business he chose as a career. He had a beautiful home and a wonderful family, but something seemed to be missing. He began to think about his father, whom he had not seen or talked to since his graduation day. He decided he should go to see his father, who was getting up in years.

Before he was able to make arrangements to go, he received a call from a funeral director, telling him that his father had passed away. He was told that his father had willed all his possessions to him and that he needed to come home and take care of things. With sadness and a lot of regret, he made his way to his dad's home.

As he went through his father's important documents, he saw the bible his father had given him for graduation years earlier. The bible looked new, just like it had years earlier when it had been given to him. With tears in his eyes, he opened the bible and began to thumb through the pages. He saw where his father had carefully underlined a verse: "If you then, being evil, know how to give good gifts to your children, how much more will your Father who is in heaven give good things to those who ask Him" (Matthew 7:11, NKJV).

As the son read these words, a car key dropped from the back of the bible. It had a tag on it with the car dealer's name, the same dealer who had the sports car that he had wanted so badly for his college graduation gift. On the tag was the date of his graduation and the words written in large print "Paid in full." The young man had accepted the gift but he had never received the content of the gift.

Here is the unvarnished truth: Even though we have accepted God's gift, we are not enjoying what we have been given because we have never opened it. We know very little about what we have that is inside the container. What did we receive when we accepted Jesus as our personal Lord and Savior? We need to open the gift, so we can start enjoying the contents. Once we begin to discover the contents of the gift, our birthright privileges, we must never allow the content to become more important to us than the gift itself.

If we only knew that a gift is a container with content.

If We Only Knew
We're More Than Conquerors

Their Name Could Be Called Legion

IT WAS A SURREAL MOMENT. I WAS SITTING FACE-TO-FACE CHATTING with an individual I had watched on television for many years. This person's worship music has blessed untold numbers of people all around the world. The chances are good that most who are reading this, have some worship CDs this individual has produced. I think I may have them all.

This person's ingratiating smile was gradually replaced with a drawn, tormented scowl as they shared their story. The individual had been caught having an extramarital affair. This was not the first one, either. The person's board of directors had insisted the individual step down from ministry and get help. You can imagine the pain, hurt, and humiliation the person's family and friends were going through. I could call this person's name Legion because they are many. This story is one I have heard more times than I care to remember.

A pastor friend and I spent an entire day ministering to this individual. We took the person through deliverance and the exchanged

9

life. There were moments during our ministry time when the light of revelation would come on as we talked about our identities as new creations. But when it was all said and done, the individual returned to his/her home state and continued with the adulterous affair.

Deception is a formidable foe. The reason deception is so dangerous, is because it is so deceiving. Hello. The enemy of our souls will try to convince us that what we are crying out for can be found in something or someone other than the Lord. When we fall for this lie, we are susceptible to all kinds of missteps. Our choices can have severe consequences as well. Everything this person was longing for and dreaming about, this person already had in Jesus. The individual had accepted God's gift but had not received the content of that gift. As a believer, the person was going to heaven but were not having a heavenly time getting there. What this individual thought was love, was really lust.

It is possible to start thinking something is right even when we know it is wrong. It makes it a lot easier to become a victim of the enemy's scam when we do not know our identity in Christ.

More Than a Conqueror

The word of God does not say that we are conquerors. It says that we are *more than* conquerors. More than a conqueror? Most of us would settle with a tie every now and then. To be more than a conqueror is incomprehensible to most of us. No matter what the enemy uses to entice us with, we have overwhelming victory in Christ. "We are *more than conquerors* through Him who loves us" (Romans 8:37, NKJV; emphasis added). It does not matter how strong the competition is or what the world may throw at us; we can come out as winners every time. A child of God should never get tired of winning. It is easy to become a victim if we do not know that Christ has already made us a victor. "We are all born ignorant, but one must work hard to remain ignorant" (Ben Franklin). The reason we sometimes make unwise choices is because of a lack of knowledge about our identities as children of God. Why is the Legion testimony that we began this chapter with so common within the family of faith? If we are more than conquerors in Christ, then why are we being conquered by our failures? Maybe it is because we really do not know what we think we know. Where do we begin? Let's begin with the following.

- We live our new-creation life by the life of another "I have been crucified with Christ, it is no longer I who live but Christ lives in me; and the life which I now live in the flesh I live by faith in (of) the Son of God who loved me and gave Himself for me" (Galatians 2:20, NKJV). The person we used to be was crucified with Christ. That person no longer lives. When Christ arose from the dead, our new selves rose with Him. Our old selves were not raised, because God cannot and will not cohabit with sin. Christ now lives His life through the new us, as us. When the tempter rings your door bell, tell Jesus it is for Him. He will be more than happy to answer the door for you.
- Christ is the anchor of our souls. "This hope we have as an *anchor of the soul* both sure and steadfast and which enters the Presence behind the veil" (Hebrews 6:19, NKJV; emphasis added). What does an anchor do for a ship? It does not keep storms from coming, but it does steady the ship in the midst of the storm. As long as we are in this world, we will have challenges. There will be fierce temptation storms. These storms are inevitable because we are in this world. What we need to remember is that *we are not of this world*. When the storms of life hit, we have a sure anchor to steady us. The next time you find yourself in a storm, trust your anchor. Place your focus on the anchor, not on the storm.
- Our existence depends entirely upon Christ. He is our environment for surviving and thriving. "For *in Him* we live and move and have our being" (Acts 17:28, NKJV; emphasis

added). Like a fish lives, moves, and enjoys its freedom in water, we find our life and freedom in Christ. Far too many believers are living their lives like a fish out of water. We know how stinky and messy that can be. We were created by Him, for Him, to live in Him, and have Him live His life in and through us. In Him we live, move, and have our very existence. The next time you have thoughts about taking a bite of the bait the tempter dangles before you, try to imagine the smell of a fish out of water.

- We are dead to sin. "Likewise you also, *reckon yourselves to be dead indeed to sin* but alive to God in Christ Jesus our Lord" (Romans 6:11, NKJV; emphasis added). We may find it difficult to reckon something we do not know. Paul tells us that we are no longer slaves to sin. The old person was crucified with Christ. Sin is not attractive to a dead person. "For *he who has died* has been *freed from sin*" (Romans 6:7, NKJV; emphasis added). Sin is not dead to us; we are dead to sin. Here is an example of what I am talking about: I have a total disdain for liver. I do not like liver, and I do not like people who like liver. I am overstating the part about not liking people who like liver. Liver is not dead to me; I am dead to liver! That should be our position when it comes to sin. We should think about sin the way God thinks about sin. He has total contempt for it. When we think about sin the way God thinks about it, we will find ourselves sinning less. The next time temptation comes creeping around your door, remind yourself that you are dead to sin. Dead people don't eat.

Knowing What You Don't Know

Confucius said, "To know what you know and what you do not know, that is true knowledge." Confucius doesn't sound confused to me. What is it that keeps us from enjoying more than a conquerors life? *Maybe we don't know what we don't know.* It just may be that we have never even thought about what we do not know, what we have in Christ. If that is the case, it can be rectified. Jesus said that if we make ourselves at home in His word, we will know the truth, and the truth we know will make and keep us free. "Then Jesus said to those Jews who believed in Him, 'If you *abide in my word*, you are my disciples indeed. And *you shall know the truth*, and the truth shall make you free'" (John 8:31–32, NKJV; emphasis added). Truth is truth whether you are free or not. Jesus says that it is the truth you know that sets you free. The truth you know will also keep you free. The key to living more than a conqueror's life is to make ourselves at home in the word of God. The more time we spend in God's word, the more we will learn what we do not know. When you spend time in God's word, you will discover that Christ has made you more than a conqueror.

In Paul's letter to the Christians who lived in Rome, he asked them this question: Is there anything that can separate us from the love of God? When we find ourselves going through difficult times, does that mean God no longer loves us? Paul should know a little something about life's battles. His life after accepting Jesus Christ as his Lord and Savior was one life-threatening event after another. Remember, Paul is the one who said that we are more than conquerors in Christ. He has been there and done that. He has the shirt, the hat, and the diploma from the university of hard knocks to prove it. Paul said that nothing can separate us from the love of God. "Can anything separate us from Christ's love? Does it mean that God no longer loves us if we have trouble or calamity, or are persecuted, or hungry, or destitute, or in danger or threatened with death? (As the Scriptures say, For your sake we are killed every day; we are being slaughtered like sheep.) No, despite all these things, overwhelming victory is ours through Christ, who loved us" (Romans 8:35–37, NLT). Just by the sheer fact that we are in this world exposes us to times of uncertainty. Despite all these things, we are still more than conquerors in Christ.

The enemy wants us to question God's love for us when we find ourselves going through difficult times. Untrue thoughts like this can creep into our heads, "If God loves you so much, why has He allowed this to happen to you?" Being a child of God does not exempt us from going through difficult times or inoculate us from danger. For us to live as conquerors, we must be convinced that God's love for us is unconditional and that it never wavers. Paul was persuaded. "For I am persuaded that neither death nor life, nor angels nor principalities nor powers, nor things present nor things to come, nor height nor depth, nor any other created thing, shall be able to separate us from the love of God which is in Christ Jesus our Lord" (Romans 8:38–39, NKJV). Paul was convinced that nothing, absolutely nothing, could separate him from the love of God. Paul was convinced that God loved him even when things looked like they were falling apart. For us to reign in this life, especially during the most difficult times, we have to be convinced that God is with us and that His love for us is unfailing.

Paul said that he was convinced there is nothing in the present or future that can separate us from the love of God. I find it interesting that Paul does not mention the past. The past is usually what the enemy uses in his attempt to keep us from living a victorious life. He is good at reminding us of all the failures of our past. There is not a thing we can do about our pasts, and the enemy knows it. We cannot go back in time and redo it. Could it be that the enemy of our souls knows something that we do not know? Maybe there is something that can be done about our pasts. We can exchange our old identities for new identities, our old natures for new ones. This is exactly what happened when we had our born from above experience. When you accepted the Lord's invitation to life, and you received Him as your Lord and Savior, you were given eternal life. Something that is eternal has no beginning. If it had a beginning it could not be eternal. God is eternal. He has no beginning. Since our new nature is eternal, our new nature has no beginning, therefore, the new creation has no past. The grace of God takes you from being a victim to being a victor. He makes you more than a conqueror.

The Mentality of a Conqueror

Bad choices can create consequences that we may have to deal with, some for the rest of our lives on this earth. The beautiful thing about living as a conqueror, we can deal with the consequences from our past mistakes in the light of who Christ has made us to be, and not who we use to be. Bad choices that we make as new creations in Christ may also have long term consequences as well. When we become convinced of who we are in Christ, we do not become sinless, but we will sin less.

As conquerors, we acknowledge facts, but we confess the truth. Pretending something is not real or that it does not exist, is not a mark of spiritual maturity. It is having an ostrich mentality. It is refusing to face reality or to acknowledge the facts. Sticking one's head in the sand, thinking all is well when things are not well, is not living the more than a conqueror life. It is actually the opposite. Acknowledging facts is not, I repeat, is not a demonstration of a lack of faith. Facts are real but facts may not be true. We may be given a medical report that is based on facts. It is okay to acknowledge that report, but as a believer, we have the choice to believe another report. It is a report based on the truth. "By His stripes we are healed" (Isaiah 53:5; 1 Peter 2:24 NKJV). Truth will always trump facts.

The Greek word *confess* means to say the same thing. Confessing truth is to say the same thing that God says about something. This is why it is imperative that we spend time in the word of God, which Jesus calls truth (John 17:17, NKJV). We will know the truth and the truth we know will set us free, and the truth we know will keep us free.

James tells us that troubles are inevitable (James 1:2, NKJV). It is not if troubles come, it is when troubles come. We live in a world that has been contaminated by sin. Adam's fall affected us all. As long as we are in this world we will have to go through some difficult times. But we do not have to be conquered by them if we have the mentality of a conqueror.

Paul addresses the more than a conqueror mentality in his second letter to the Family of Faith living in Corinth. "We are pressed on every side by troubles, but we are not crushed. We are perplexed, but not driven to despair. We are hunted down, but never abandoned by God. We get knocked down but we are not destroyed" (2 Corinthians 4:8–9, NLT). How can a person have such an incredible attitude while going through tough times? Keep reading. "That is why we never give up. Though our bodies are dying, our spirits are being renewed every day. For our present troubles are small and won't last very long. Yet they produce for us a glory that vastly outweighs them and will last forever! So we don't look at the troubles we can see now *[facts]*; rather, we fix our gaze on things that cannot be seen *[truth]*. For the things we see now *[facts]* will soon be gone, but the things we cannot see *[truth]* will last forever" (2 Corinthians 4:16–18, NLT; emphasis added). Paul is telling us what a conqueror's mentality is as they look at life. We do not deny what we are going through, but we are going through. Our God is bigger than any circumstance or situation that we may find ourselves in. A more than a conqueror does not tell God how big their problems are, a more than a conqueror tells their problems how big their God is. This is the truth!

A more than a conqueror refuses to go along, just to get along. In the book of Daniel, we read the testimony of three men, Shadrach, Meshach, and Abed-Nego, who refused to bow down and worship an idol. Their love for God and loyalty to Him was stronger than their will to live. When King Nebuchadnezzar gave them the opportunity to change their mind and submit, they did not hesitate or blink. Shadrach, Meshach, and Abed-Nego, immediately went on record. "Let it be known to you, O king, that we do not serve your gods, nor will we worship the gold image which you have set up" (Daniel 3:18, NKJV). These three men refused to go along, just to get along. This is the more than a conqueror mentality.

Jesus said, "I have told you all this so that *you may have peace in me*. Here on earth you will have many trials and sorrows. But take heart because *I have overcome the world*" (John, 16:33 NLTV; emphasis added). Again, we are told that as long as we are in this world, we will go through some difficult times. Trials and sorrows are like death and taxes, they are inevitable. Jesus says a couple of things in this verse that we need to pay close attention to. The first thing is the only place we can find peace is in Christ. Christ is or peace (Ephesians 2:14, NKJV). He is not one of many places where we can find peace, Christ is the only place where we can find peace. The second thing is, Jesus said that He has already overcome the world. He did not say that He will conquer the world, He said that He has already conquered the world. Let that sink in for a moment. Jesus has not yet gone through the Garden of Gethsemane experience yet, He has not gone through all the ridiculing, mocking, being spit on, tortured, and ultimately nailed to a tree. Judas had not yet sold Him out for thirty pieces of silver. Jesus said that He had already overcome the world before all of His disciples had deserted Him. How could He say something that sounds so far-fetched? Could it be that He knew the Lamb had been slain before the foundation of the world (Revelation 13:8, NKJV)? God took care of every problem outside of time before there was ever a problem in time. This is crucial in our understanding of how it is possible to go through tough times with the mental attitude of a more than a conqueror. We have already won before we even knew we have a need to win. We do not become more than a conqueror during our conflicts, we go in to our conflicts as more than a conqueror. We win because Christ has won.

The first school I attended was for grades one through twelve. It was a country school called Rice Elementary. At recess time, we would go outside to a designated area to play. Sometimes the high school kids would be having their break when we had ours. They looked like adults to a first-grader. We were more than happy to keep our distance.

We had a special game we enjoyed playing as boys. We called it *horse*. One boy would sit on the shoulders of another boy, and we would see who could pull the other teams down to the ground, or cause them to fall. The last one standing was declared the champion. I don't think I ever lost a contest. I may have and just can't remember, or don't want to admit it. That is my story anyway and I am sticking to it. My victories were gained, not because of my size or from my strength. I was victorious because of the size and strength of my horse. Doug Smith would always be my horse. He was so much bigger than most of the other first-graders. Doug liked carrying me on his shoulders because I was smaller than most of the other kids. I liked Doug being my horse, because he was big and strong. I was able to win because of the strength that was under me, not because of the strength that was in me.

We are more than a conqueror because of Christ being in us, not because of anything else. This is the truth that sets us free and it is the truth that will keep us free.

If we only knew that Christ has made us more than a conqueror.

If We Only Knew

It Is Hard to Live like a Son if You Think like a Slave

In the fifteenth chapter of Luke, Jesus tells us the story about a father who had two sons. "The younger son told his father, 'I want my share of your estate now before you die'" (Luke 15:12, NLT). To make this demand while his father was living was equivalent to saying, "I wish you were dead." What in the world was he thinking? He had already left home in his mind and was on the verge of taking his first step down the road that has no end.

A few days later, he packed his bag and left home. The pouch strapped firmly around his waist was full of money. He was on his way to *find himself*. Dressed like a millionaire playboy, he was on his way to living the good life, a life of his own choosing. Freedom! There would be no one telling him what he could or could not do. He was now a free man. From that time forward, he would be calling his own shots. I wonder what song he was singing as he headed toward the far country. Who knows, but I can envision him singing louder and louder as his father's home grew smaller and smaller behind him, while the lights of the big city were growing bigger and bigger in front of him. Look out world, here he comes.

A Parable with Three Windows

Some people see three parables in the fifteenth chapter of Luke. I see one parable that has three windows that allow us to see into the same truth from three different angles. What is a parable? Jesus was a master teacher, and He would often use a parable to communicate a truth He wanted His hearers to understand. A parable is an earthly story that has a heavenly meaning. The Greek word is *parabole*. It means to place something alongside something else with an intent to compare. It is to take an earthly story and lay it down or place it beside truth. Once you understand the story, you will grasp the truth that it is conveying. There are two dangers we need to avoid when it comes to interrupting a parable. The first one is to ignore important features, and the second one is to try making every detail mean something.

The three stories Jesus tells in Luke 15 are windows that helps us see the truth of how the Father feels about us, and what He thinks of us. When we understand the meaning of the story, we will begin to understand how much our heavenly Father loves us. The first window of this parable is about a man who has one hundred sheep, and one goes astray. It wanders away from the flock and finds itself lost. The second window of this parable is about a woman who has ten pieces of silver. She loses one of them. One piece of silver is lost. The third window of this parable is about a father who has two sons. One leaves home and finds himself lost. There is one thing that ties these three stories together. There is a big celebration when that which was lost is found.

We have the lost sheep, the lost silver, and the lost son. The sheep was lost and knew it, but it did not know how to return to the flock. The shepherd went in search of the sheep, found it, and bought it back to where it belonged. Once the sheep was back in its place, there was a big celebration. The piece of silver was lost and did not know it. How can a piece of silver know anything? The woman diligently searched for it until it was found. The piece of silver was put back in its rightful place. She invited her friends and neighbors over for a party. The son was lost, and he knew it. Unlike the sheep and the silver, the son knew how to get back to where he belonged. His father threw a huge party to celebrate his son's return. The celebration over what was once out of place but is now back in place is what ties these three window frames together; making it one parable.

Every Play Day Has a Pay Day

Having a life with no boundaries, no authority figures telling you what you can or cannot do is fantastic—for a season. With every play day comes a pay day. Jesus said that this young man wasted his money on prodigal living. He was wastefully extravagant with his spending. He was reckless and careless. I am sure he was surrounded by several enthusiastic party friends, who were telling him how wonderful he was—as long as he was buying the rounds. He had this "adulting thing" down. Later, we find out from the elder son that this boy had wasted his livelihood on harlots. I will leave that to your own imagination.

"When he had spent all." These are the words of Jesus (Luke 15:14, NKJV). It is now pay day. This is the only outcome when we choose to live outside the boundaries. What appears to be freedom may actually be bondage. Rebellion often disguises itself as freedom. Always remember, every play day has a pay day. "Sin will take you farther than you want to go, keep you much longer than you want to stay, and cost you far more than you want to pay" (R. Zaccharias).

Cheer Up—Things Can Get Worse

When this young man comes to the end of his rope, a severe famine hits the land—a double whammy. Jesus said that no one gave him anything. Where are all those party friends, the ones who were telling him how wonderful he was? Probably patting someone else on the back and telling them how great they were, now that they were the ones buying the drinks.

With no money, no friends, and no help, he found himself doing something that he probably had said he would never do. He hired himself out to be a keeper of pigs. This is the first indication that this son is beginning to think like a slave. It was during this worst of times that he had his *come-to-the-father moment*. Sometimes it takes coming to the end of ourselves to realize what we really need. When we end up with absolutely nothing but Jesus, we discover that we have just enough to start over.

One day, while watching the pigs, his hunger pains were so severe that it almost drove him to eat the pods the pigs were eating. Suddenly, he snapped. He began to think in a sensible way. Jesus said, "He came to his senses" (Luke 15:17, NLT; emphasis added). He began to think about his father and the freedoms he enjoyed while living in his father's home. Yes, freedom. He thought about all the servants his father had and how well they were taken care of. As servants, they had plenty to eat; as a son, he was on the verge of starving. He was beginning to realize that he was out of place by choice.

Thinking like a Slave

He begins to talk to himself. "I will arise and go to my father and will say to him, 'Father, I have sinned against heaven and before you, and *I am no longer worthy to be called your son. Make me like one of your hired servants*'" (Luke 15:18–19, NKJV; emphasis added). It is hard to live like a son when you think like a slave. His heart turned toward home and his body followed. He did not feel worthy to be called a son, but he would settle with being called a servant.

Try to picture in your mind what he must have looked like. What a contrast to what he looked like when he had walked away from his father. He stank! He had been with pigs. The clothes he had on his back were torn and soiled. His feet were bare because he had either lost his shoes or hocked them at a local far country pawn shop. The outside of him could not even begin to compare with the mess that was on the inside of him. I am sure there were times during his long walk home when he had to fight the urge to turn around. What would his father say to him? Would he be rejected and turned away? Surely, he would be given a stern lecture about the choices he made and their consequences. After all, he had wished his father was dead by asking for a portion of his father's wealth. How would his father see him now? How would he feel about him?

The Father's Heart Revealed

While he was still a long way off, his father saw him coming. To the son's utter amazement, he saw his father running toward him. We can only imagine the kaleidoscope of thoughts and feelings that must have been flooding though his head as his father came closer and closer. "Is he racing toward me to turn me away? Here comes the lecture! Here comes the I-told-you-so sermon,'" he likely said to himself. Was this young man in for a shock! When his father reached him, he grabbed him with both arms and began to kiss him repetitively. The son began to deliver the speech he had prepared. "Father, I have sinned against heaven and in your sight and am no longer worthy to be called your son" (Luke 15:21, NKJV). But he was unable to finish his prepared speech. The words, *make me one of your servants* never came out of his mouth, because his father was hugging him so tight and kissing him so fast. The father never responded to what his son said. It was almost as if he did not hear him. He told the servants, "Let's get the party started." Even though the son was thinking like a slave, the father treated him like a son. Why? Because he was his father's son. This was the only way the father could treat him.

Homecoming Gifts

The father told the servants to put *the best robe* on his son; not just any robe would do. It had to be the best robe. Isn't it interesting that he was not instructed to take a bath and clean up before the robe could be worn? The robe covered the sin-soiled garments he was wearing. He was given a ring to wear on his hand. This ring was the family credit card. The imprint of the family ring was the official seal of a business transaction. Wait a minute. He had wasted his livelihood, and his father has given him access to the family treasury—again. He puts sandals on his son's feet. Lord knows what happened to his old ones. A slave did not wear shoes. This young man was given shoes because he was the father's son, not one of his servants. Then they killed the fatted calf and celebrated, for the son who was dead was now alive; he was lost but now he had been found. The son was back in the father's house where he belonged.

There is one very important element to this story that is easy to overlook. It is so liberating too. The prodigal son wasted his livelihood, but he did not lose his inheritance. Neither did the individual we called Legion in chapter 2. That person finally came to one's senses, just like the prodigal son did, and returned to the Father. The individual wasted the livelihood but did not lose the inheritance. Today, this individual is actively engaged in ministry, blessing untold numbers of people. It is hard to live like a son if you think like a slave.

The following is a snippet from "The Father's Bargain," written by Puritan John Flavel (1627–1691). It is an imagined conversation that God, the Father, is having with His Son, Jesus, about effectual grace. You and I are included in this conversation.

> Father: My son, here is a company of poor miserable souls, that have utterly undone themselves, and now lie open to my justice! Justice demands satisfaction for them, or will satisfy itself in the eternal ruin of them: What shall be done for these souls?

Son: O my Father, such is my love to, and pity for them, that rather than they shall perish eternally, I will be responsible for them as their Surety; bring in all thy bills, that I may see what they owe thee; Lord, bring them all in that there may be no after-reckonings with them; at my hand shalt thou require it. I will rather choose to suffer thy wrath than they should suffer it: upon me, my Father, upon me be all their debt.

Father: But, my Son, if thou undertake for them, thou must reckon to pay the last mite, expect no abatements; if I spare them, I will not spare thee.

Son: Content, Father, let it be so; charge it all upon me, I am able to discharge it: and though it prove a kind of undoing to me, though it impoverish all my riches, empty all my treasures, (for so indeed it did 2 Corinthians 8:9 NKJV). "Though he was rich, yet for our sakes he became poor") yet I am content to undertake it.

Flavel: Blush, ungrateful believers, O let shame cover your faces; judge in yourselves now, has Christ deserved that you should stand with him for trifles, that you should shrink at a few petty difficulties, and complain, this is hard, and that is harsh? O if you knew the grace of our Lord Jesus Christ in this his wonderful condescension for you, you could not do it.

Can you imagine how our heavenly Father must have felt knowing that His Son would take our place on the cross, that he would shed His blood for your sins and mine, and that He would die the death we deserved? Jesus was willing to pay for all our sins, past, present, and future, by sacrificing His life on an old rugged cross. How good is that? This is the heart and soul of the story of the father and his wayward son, told by Jesus in Luke 15 (NKJV). It is the message of grace. There is more grace in Him than there is sin in any of us.

I know there are those who say that the message of grace will give people a license to sin. Someone who really believes that does not have a healthy understanding of grace. Have you noticed that people do not need a license to sin? The message of grace does not give us a license to sin; grace gives us the freedom and liberty of not wanting to sin. Grace changes our *want-tos*!

If we only knew how our heavenly Father feels and thinks about us, even when we make bad decisions, we would not run away from Him: We would be running to Him. He remains approachable, accessible, and available to His children.

4

If We Only Knew
The Gift of Living Water

ONE DAY, OUT OF CURIOSITY, I GOOGLED TO SEE IF I COULD FIND out who held the record for being married the most times. My search led me to a person who had been married twenty-nine times. That's what I thought too. Twenty-nine times! The person's shortest marriage lasted nineteen days, while the longest marriage lasted eleven years. This individual changed marriage partners almost more often than the person changed clothes. It does not take a marriage counselor to know what the main ingredient is in all those failed marriages. They all have one thing in common. See if you can figure it out.

Empty Pot Empty Life

She came to draw water in the heat of the noonday sun like she did every day—alone. The only steady companion she had was her water pot. She and her water pot had something in common: they were both empty. Every day, she would make that walk to Jacob's well to refill the pot. The pot would soon be empty again, and so back to the well she would go. Physical thirst is constant and it must be satisfied, or there can be grave consequences. This woman's physical survival was dependent on the well water.

This lady was living with a man who was not her husband. She'd had five failed marriages before she was in this live-in relationship. She was not going to risk another failed marriage and all the pain that came with it. That says a lot about what her empty soul was crying out for. She just wanted someone to love her unconditionally and to be her covenant partner. She tried to fill that empty spot in her soul by going to the marriage well five times. Why risk a sixth marriage? Just live together instead, because it is a pretty sure bet that this one will not work out either. This way, the separation will be somewhat easier and the fallout less painful.

Her focus was on getting her physical needs met and neglected her spiritual needs. The water in the well could satisfy only her physical thirst. Jesus is the only one who could satisfy her spiritual thirst. Jesus told her, "Whoever drinks of this water [well] will thirst again. But whoever drinks of the water that I shall give him will never thirst. But the water that I shall give him will become in him a fountain of water springing up into everlasting life" (John 4:13–14, NKJV; emphasis added). I love Dr. Theodore Isaac Rubin's quote, "The problem is not that there are problems. The problem is expecting otherwise and thinking that having problems is a problem." The Samaritan woman thought her problem was that she could not find the right soul mate. What she thought was her problem, was not her actual problem—and that was her problem. It is like changing a tire on your vehicle so it will start, when you actually need to fill the gas tank because it is empty. She was looking for love in all the wrong places.

Teaching by Apperception

Apperception is a teaching method that uses something that someone is familiar with to teach them about something they know nothing about. Jesus was a master with this teaching method. This Samaritan woman knew something about the water that was inside the well. She knew it would take care of her physical needs, but she knew nothing whatsoever about the Living Water that would take care of her spiritual needs.

What this woman was searching for could not be found in Jacob's well or in five marriages. The temporary relief she would get from the well would be just that, temporary. Little did she know that what she was looking for would be found in the man sitting on the curb beside the well. The seventh man would totally transform her life. She would find what she had always been looking for in Him. Jesus told a group of sign seekers, "I am the bread of life. He who comes to Me shall *never hunger,* and he who believes in Me shall *never thirst*" (John 6:35, NKJV; emphasis added). Jesus is the only one who can totally satisfy the longing that is in a person's innermost being.

She Left Her Empty Water Pot

After their conversation about worship, Jesus comes right out and tells her that He is the Messiah. "I who speak to you am He" (John 4:26, NKJV). Her reaction was amazing. She left her empty water pot and ran back in to the city, screaming at the top of her lungs, "Come, see the Man who told me all things that I ever did. Could this be the Messiah?" (John 4:29, NKJV). Do not overlook what she left behind: her constant companion, the water pot. It was still empty, but she was full of living water. Jesus was able to do what the water in the well could never do, satisfy her spiritual thirst. She would never thirst again. Once our spiritual needs are met, we will not be driven and controlled by our physical needs.

God does choose the most unlikely to confound the wise, doesn't He (1 Corinthians 2:2–29, NKJV)? Who would have chosen a woman who had been married five times, and who was living with another man, to be a messenger of the good news? I do not think many churches would put their stamp of approval on such an individual. We are told that many Samaritans believed in Jesus because of this woman's testimony (John 4:39, NKJV).

I think it is interesting that this woman is not named. She is just referred to as the Samaritan woman. Could it be that it is intentional? By not naming her, we can insert our own names. Her story could be our stories. Most of us have been duped into thinking that the deep cry of our souls can be satisfied by the acquisition of things or by having the right person in our lives. If that is our pursuit, then we will be left empty just like the woman's water pot. Trips to the water well will never end because physical water can never quench our spiritual thirst.

The Samaritan woman now knows what Jesus meant when He said, "*If you only knew* the gift that God has for you, and to whom you are speaking, you would ask Me and I would give you living water" (John 4:10, NKJV; emphasis added). What was true then is true now. Everything the human soul is searching for can be found only in Jesus.

In his letter to the church a Colossi, Paul writes, "Christ is our life" (Colossians 3:4, NKJV). This is exactly what Luke said in the book of Acts. "In Him (Christ) we live and move and have our being" (Acts 17:28, NKJV). Christ is the only environment humanity can find survival in. If we try to find life in anything or in anyone else, we will live in a perpetual state of spiritual thirst. It is impossible to draw enough water from the world's well to satisfy the thirst of a parched soul.

Why Settle for Well Water When We Can Have Living Water?

We could describe well water as materialism. Materialism is an insidious system that is governed by money, which is the god of this world. The bible does not say that money is the root of all evil; it says *the love for money* is the root of all evil. "For the love of money is the root of all kinds of evil. And some people, craving money, have wandered from the true faith and pierced themselves with many sorrows" (1 Timothy 6:10, NLT). Material possessions do offer temporary security but no ultimate serenity.

Materialism is a very addictive drug. How much is enough? Possessions do have value, but when left unchecked, their value begins to possess us. "He who loves silver will not be satisfied with silver; nor he who loves abundance with increase. This also is vanity" (Ecclesiastes 5:10, NKJV). A parched soul can never have enough stuff to satisfy its thirst. Those who love money will never have enough. Jesus said, "And what do you benefit if you gain the whole world but lose your own soul?" (Matthew 16:26, NLT). It is OK to have things, so long as things do not have you.

The only inoculation for materialism addiction is living water—Jesus. This is exactly what Jesus told the Samaritan woman who came to draw more water from the well. Her life was as empty as her five previous marriages were, her present live-in relationship, and her water pot. *"If you knew the gift of God,* and who it is who says to you, 'Give me a drink,' you would asked Him, and He would have given you *living water"* (John 4:10, NKJV; emphasis added). What did Jesus mean by living water? Don't we need water to survive? Of course we do. A human cannot live more than three to four days without water.

Jesus was not denying her need for physical water. He was revealing that her need for physical water was not as important as her need was for spiritual water, living water. Jesus used her physical need to reveal her spiritual need. The physical is temporary, while the spiritual is eternal. Spiritual thirst is far greater than physical thirst. Once we get our spiritual thirst satisfied, our physical wants become less important. After all, we are not physical beings having a temporary spiritual experience. We are spiritual beings having a temporary physical experience.

Jesus tells a story about two men in the gospel of Luke. One was a certain rich man who had plenty of the world's possessions, and the other one he called by name, Lazarus. Lazarus was very poor and had to beg for scraps to eat. He was covered with sores and lay daily at the rich man's gate, where he begged for food. The stray dogs showed more compassion on him than the rich man did.

Finally, they both died. Have you noticed that death is no respecter of person? It does not matter if you have an abundance of material possessions or if you are destitute; death is a common denominator. Death comes once per person. Where a person spends eternity is decided on this side of death. Death took Lazarus into the presence of the Lord, but death separated the rich man from the presence of the Lord. What determined their destinies? Lazarus did not go to heaven because he was poor any more than the rich man went to hell because he was rich. The rich man had plenty of well water to drink. He had no lack when it came to physical possessions, but he was spiritually destitute. Lazarus was destitute when it came to physical possessions, but he was spiritually rich because he drank from the living water. The physical is temporary, but the spiritual is eternal.

Listen to what Jesus said about the rich man. "The rich man shouted, 'Father Abraham, have some pity! Send Lazarus over here to *dip the tip of his finger in water and cool my tongue.* I am in anguish in these flames'" (Luke 16:24, NKJV; emphasis added). Who is thirsty now? Who is begging now? The reason this is so sad is because it is totally avoidable. This gift of living water is still being offered to all those who are thirsty. It is available for the up-and-out as well as the down-and-out and to the in-and-out. Whosoever will, may come and drink freely. "And the Spirit and the bride say, 'Come!' And let him who hears say, 'Come!' And *let him who thirsts come.* Whoever desires, let him take of the water of life freely" (Revelation 22:17, NKJV; emphasis added).

People are burning themselves out trying to fill the void they feel in their lives. Unfortunately, they are trying to fill it with things that cannot satisfy. They end up feeling even emptier. It is like drinking seawater. "The more you drink, the thirstier you become" (Arthur Schopenhauer).

We were all born with an empty spot deep within us that only God can fill. This is why anyone without Christ is incomplete. "*So you are complete through your union with Christ,* who is the head over every ruler and authority" (Colossians 2:10, NLT; emphasis added). Blaise Pascal (1623–1662), the Catholic theologian, said, "There is a God-shaped vacuum in the heart of each man which cannot be satisfied by any created thing, but only by God the Creator, made known through Jesus Christ."

Someone falsely reported that the following are the last words of billionaire Steve Jobs, cofounder of Apple, but it has been proven they are not. But these could be the last words spoken by anyone on his or her death bed who has found the true meaning of living life. "At this moment, lying on a sick bed and recalling my whole life, I realize that all the recognition and material possessions that I took so much pride in have paled and become meaningless in the face of impending death. You can employ someone to drive the car for you, make money for you, but you cannot have someone to bear the sickness for you. Material things lost can be found. But there is one thing that can never be found when it is lost, life." Truer words have never been spoken.

Jesus is God's gift to us. *If we only knew* the gift of living water.

If We Only Knew

All Things Are
HIM-possible

I FIND IT INSPIRING TO BE AROUND PEOPLE WHO HAVE POSITIVE attitudes. Someone who is optimistic about life will usually succeed where others fail. It is refreshing to associate with people who are confident and cheerful. This is why I try to surround myself with people who choose to see the upside to every downside. Confidence can sometimes be misconstrued as conceit. Just because someone believes he or she can do something does not necessarily mean this person is self-centered.

I read a little maxim once that has been a huge encouragement to me over the years. It goes like this: "It is your *attitude*, not your *aptitude*, that determines your *altitude*." My rendition of this apothegm is, "How high you fly in this life will be determined by your attitude, not by how smart you are."

We must never be hoodwinked into thinking that a positive attitude can replace faith. I know many people who are not Christians who have incredibly positive attitudes. As wonderful as it is to have a good attitude, it can never be substituted for faith. The fruit of faith should be a good attitude, but faith is not the fruit of a good attitude. The bible does not say that a good attitude pleases the Lord. The word says that without faith, it is impossible to please the Lord (Hebrews 11:6, NKJV).

The apostle Paul had a great attitude. Several of his letters to the church were written while he was in prison. His attitude was so positive that we never would have known his circumstances if he had not told us. From a prison cell, he writes, "I can do all things through Christ who strengthens me" (Philippians 4:13, NKJV). Paul is not saying that there is nothing he cannot do. He is saying that, with Christ, all things are Him-possible. This declaration of being able to do all things through Christ is his response to the concern the church at Philippi had for him. He thanked them for being sensitive about his welfare. It was a comfort for him to know that the church family at Philippi wanted him to fare well. He fully understood they did not have the means to provide him with assistance at times. He tells them that he has learned how to be content no matter what life throws at him. He knows how to exist on plenty and how to get by on a little. Sometimes his stomach was full, and sometimes it was empty. It really did not matter what his circumstances were, because he had learned that he could do anything with Christ's help. Life had taught him so much about what faith is. Faith is not about everything turning out all right. It is about being all right no matter how things turn out. All things are HIM-possible.

The ability to do all things through Christ does not mean you can be a brain surgeon, even though you scored a 2 on your ACT. That is not what Paul is talking about. His confidence is in Christ and in His ability to get him through whatever he finds himself going through. No matter how difficult or challenging one's circumstances may be, with Christ, we have the strength to not only persevere, but we can press on with a good attitude. Faith centered in Christ produces a good attitude, and a good attitude—not how smart we may be—is what determines how high we soar in this life.

With Men, with God

Many years ago, I stood on the dock at the Port of Houston, gawking at the humongous ships anchored to the dock. This country boy had come to town. I had seen plenty of boats in my lifetime, but I had never seen a ship that was not in a magazine. Some of these ships were enormous. I was absolutely amazed that something so big could float. How in the world did they not sink to the bottom of the ocean? If I jumped off the dock into the water, I would immediately start sinking to the bottom. My friend was talking to the wind when he tried to explain to me how a ship can stay afloat by using the buoyancy principle; if the weight of displaced water is equal to the weight of the ship, the ship floats—yada, yada, yada. I could not hear a word he was saying, because my eyes were so full of these massive vessels.

I got to see several of these ginormous vessels weigh their anchors. After they had been slowly towed out to open water, they set sail. It was fascinating. We stood there for hours talking to one another and to the folks who were taking in the sights like we were. A few of the ships that had left the port earlier could now be seen only as tiny dots on the horizon. I could totally cover up and block out the ship with my thumb. My thumb was certainly not the size of those ships, so why was this possible? Position. They were no longer in my face. I could see the vessel from a different position, and it gave me a new perspective. What was huge and imposing before, now seemed so small and insignificant.

In answering the disciple's specific question about who can be saved, Jesus responded, "*With men* this is impossible, but *with God* all things are possible" (Matthew 19:26, NKJV; emphasis added). This is a truth we need to get a grip on. This is what faith is all about. Where we choose to focus our faith will determine our positions, and our positions will determine our perspective. How we see things will be decided by who or what we place our confidence in.

When we face the challenges that life can and does throw at us, we have a choice. We can keep them in our faces and be overpowered by them, or we can put them in God's face. If our choice is to keep them in our faces, we may find ourselves as victims. By choosing to put them in God's face, we are victors because we can see our challenges from a new position. Our positions of faith now give us a new perspective. All things are now Him-possible.

Strange Bedfellows

The book of James was written to Jewish believers who had been driven from their homes and from their land. They had been scattered to the four winds. To say they were going through some very difficult times would be an understatement. In his opening remarks, James says, "Dear brothers and sisters, *when troubles come* your way, consider it an opportunity for great joy" (James 1:2, NKJV; emphasis added). James does not say *if* troubles come; he says *when* troubles come. Difficult and threatening times are inevitable. Jesus said that as long as we are in this world, we will have troubles (John 16:33, NKJV). Again, it is not a matter of if we have troubles, it is when. Then Jesus says something weird. When we are facing difficult times, we are to be of good cheer. Good cheer and troubles seem like strange bedfellows to me. How in the world is it possible to deal with troubles in a spirit of joy? Maybe this is a hyperbole. Jesus tells us how this is possible. When trouble comes, you will find your peace in Me, so, "Be of good cheer *because* I have overcome the world" (John 16:33, NKJV; emphasis added). Because He won, we win. When we place our trials and troubles in His face, we are guaranteed a win.

Do not let anyone try to convince you that your new life in Christ will be like skating on thick ice. That would be cool if it were true, but we need to heed the thin-ice warning signs. The truth of the matter is, there may be more thin ice than thick ice. We are not *of this world*, but we are certainly *in this world*. Since we are in this world, we will experience a lot of thin ice moments, so tighten up those skates.

Acknowledge the Facts, but Confess the Truth

Everything I have said in this chapter up to this point is not just someone venting cute little clichés to keep the reader's attention. It is a truth that my wife and I have had to walk out and are still walking out. This entire book, *If We Only Knew*, is actually our testimony. Like Paul, we are in the process of learning what faith is. Let me repeat something I've already said: Faith is not about things turning out all right. Faith is about being all right no matter how things turn out. Did you catch what I said? We are learning.

It all began on a Monday in the month of October in 2015. I was sitting in a waiting room while my wife was having a tissue sample taken from a lump that was found in her breast. The tissue sample would be biopsied to see if the mass was cancer. Needless to say, we were both a tad anxious.

It was not long before a lady we knew personally came walking up to me and said, "Betty Ann needs you to come back." My heart flipped over. I felt my stomach twist into a knot. An alarm went off inside of me: *This doesn't sound good,* I thought. Without saying another word, she led me back to see my wife. As I walked through the door, it was obvious she was emotionally shaken. When I leaned over and hugged her, she lost it. The doctor who had taken the tissue sample told the nurse who was assisting and my wife that he had seen a lot of cancerous tissue in his medical career, and there was no doubt in his mind that this lump, this mass in her breast, was cancer.

After innumerable tests, a consultation was set up with the oncology team. We were given the medical procedure that would be followed to treat my wife's cancer. She would receive five radiation treatments. After four weeks, they would then perform a complete mastectomy and reconstructive surgery. After another six weeks, she would be given six rounds of chemotherapy.

We were at the point of finding peace with this decision when we received word about more tests that had been done. The cancer had metastasized to her liver. The oncologist elevated the cancer she was fighting to stage four. The medical procedures they had prescribed were thrown out the window. We were told that the only thing they could do was chemotherapy in an attempt to slow the cancer down.

I cannot adequately describe the look that was on the oncologist's face when I told her we would not accept their prognosis. We were not denying the facts or her diagnosis; we chose to confess the truth. The truth is, "By His stripes we are healed" (Isaiah 53:5, NKJV; 1 Peter 2:24, NKJV). In our faces, the facts the medical team had given us were nothing short of overwhelming. Our choice was to put the facts we were given in the face of our God. In our faces, it is an impossible situation. In His face, it becomes Him-possible. We acknowledge the facts (the medical report), but we choose to confess the truth: "by His stripes we are healed."

In the five years from being diagnosed with cancer to the present, my precious wife has shown incredible courage and unshakable faith. Even after 109 chemo treatments, twenty radiation treatments, and a plethora of medications, Betty Ann Kniffen stands strong in her faith in Christ. Regardless of what some may think, her strength does not come from her faith. Her strength is Christ. Christ makes her faith strong. The validity and value of our faith is determined by the object of our faith. Faith placed in anything or in anyone other than Christ is misplaced faith. The object of my wife's faith is Christ. It is Christ and Christ alone who can keep you going when everything in you is screaming to quit. It is possible to stay in perfect peace no matter how difficult your situation may be. "You keep in perfect peace all who trust in you, all whose thoughts are fixed on you! Trust in the Lord always, for the Lord God is the eternal rock" (Isaiah 26:3–4, NLT).

I can hear the great old hymn, "On Christ the Solid Rock I Stand," being sung in my head. "My hope is built on nothing less than Jesus's blood and righteousness. I dare not trust the sweetest frame but wholly lean on Jesus name. On Christ the solid rock I stand, all other ground is sinking sand, all other ground is sinking sand" (Edward Mote). No matter what life may throw at you or how difficult things may become, you can stay on your feet when you are standing on Christ the solid rock. "With Christ all things are possible" (Matthew 19:26, NKJV).

There may be times when you feel like giving up and throwing in the proverbial towel. It can happen to the best of us. If this happens, do not get trapped in self-condemnation. Remind yourself that feelings are real, but feelings are not fundamental to faith. Feelings are constantly changing, while the truth will never change, because truth cannot change. This is why it is called truth. The truth is, with Christ, all things are Him-possible.

Remember the words of Mary Kay Ash. "If you think you can, you can. If you think you can't, you're right." *If we only knew* that with God, all things are HIM-possible.

6

If We Only Knew
We Don't Have to Smell like
What We've Been Through

AS HE WALKED INTO MY OFFICE, WE GREETED ONE ANOTHER WITH a warm handshake and a node of our heads. You could tell he was having a hard time maintaining the forced smile that was on his face. We shared a few pleasantries before his voice began to crack. Tears began to pool in the corners of his eyes. After a few minutes, his emotions erupted. He could no longer hold his composure. The hurts of his wounded spirit came out like projectile vomiting. For fifteen minutes, he poured out his guts to me.

There is one thing that hurting people share in common aside from their wounds. Hurt people have a propensity to hurt people. There is no way for anyone to go through life without being wounded. It would be easier to drive a herd of cats from Amarillo, Texas, to Lubbock, Texas, than go through life without being wounded by someone's words or actions. It is like death and taxes. It is not a matter of if we die or if we pay taxes; it is when.

Many adults are carrying wounds they received during their childhoods. To protect themselves from further hurt, they turn their focus inward. A wounded spirit makes inner vows, not knowing that they are making themselves vulnerable for more hurt. An inner vow is taking on the role of God in a particular area of our lives. When we do this, we are saying in essence, "Lord, I will handle this area of my life. You take care of the rest." An example of an inner vow would be, "No one will ever hurt me again." "I will never trust another human being as long as I live." "I will never let anyone get close to me again." Do statements like these sound familiar?

This is why people isolate themselves, even though we are created for community. We allow only a few people into our inner circles, and we keep a close eye on them because we never know when they will turn on us. It is kind of like the dude who was shipwrecked on a small, deserted island. After many years, a ship came by and rescued him. Before they departed, he took the ship's crew on a tour of his little island. He shows them the little thatched hut that he had made for his house and a little building he had built for his church. Someone asked him about another little building that was close by. He said, "That's where I used to go to church." Even though we may be by ourselves, we are never alone. We cannot escape ourselves. If we are carrying a lot of emotional wounds, life can be miserable at best. Hurt people hurt people.

Can You Pass the Smell Test?

In Daniel 3, we have the story of Shadrach, Meshach, and Abednego being thrown into a fiery furnace. Their crime was refusing to bow down and worship the golden image that King Nebuchadnezzar had made. When they were given the opportunity to change their minds, they told King Nebuchadnezzar that they would not give it a second thought. They boldly declared that their God would deliver them from the furnace. But even if He did not deliver them, they would not serve other gods; neither would they bow down and worship the golden image. In rage, the king told his men to heat the furnace seven times hotter than normal. "Then these men were bound in their coats, their trousers, their turbans, and their other garments, and were cast into the midst of the burning fiery furnace" (Daniel 3:21, NKJV). The fire was so hot that the flames leaped out and consumed the men who had carried out King Nebuchadnezzar's orders. "And these three men, Shadrach, Meshach, and Abednego, fell down bound into the midst of the burning fiery furnace" (Daniel 3:23, NKJV).

All of a sudden, the king was stunned by what he saw. Four men—not three—were walking around in the fire. "Look! I see four men loose, walking in the midst of the fire; and they are not hurt, and *the form of the fourth is like the Son of God*" (Daniel 3:25, NKJV; emphasis added). King Nebuchadnezzar had never seen the Son of God. How in the world did he recognize Him as the fourth man in the fire? He didn't. The demon that was inside of the king recognized Jesus.

Here is the bottom line to their story. "And the satraps, administrators, governors, and the king's counselors gathered together, and they saw these men on whose bodies the fire had no power; the hair of their head was not singed nor were their garments affected, and *the smell of fire was not on them*" (Daniel 3:27, NKJV; emphasis added). They did not smell like what they had just been through. The only thing that burned in the fire were the ropes that had them bound. The fire that the king tried to destroy them with, God used to deliver them. They refused to bow. They would not bend, and they did not burn. When they came through their furnace experience, they did not smell like smoke.

Life Is Full of Furnace Experiences

We never know when we are going to feel the heat from a furnace experience. But here is one thing we can be assured of: the fourth man will always be with us. Sometimes, God will deliver us from the furnace. He may choose to deliver us while we are in the furnace. At other times, He may deliver us through the furnace. But He will deliver us.

I was having a conversation with a lady a few years back who was very emotional as she talked about her failed marriage. To say she was a basket case would not adequately describe her emotional condition. Her pain and hurt had me at the point of tears. I was on the verge of losing it myself. I asked her the obvious question: "When was your divorce final?" Because of the emotional trauma she was experiencing, I assumed it was recent. When she said her divorce had been final for seventeen years, my eyes dried immediately. My sympathy for her dried up too—seventeen years! The smell of her divorce furnace was all over her. By no means am I making light of the pain a divorce can cause. A divorce can be devastating. But to carry the smell for seventeen years!

A furnace experience can be the loss of a child or a loved one. It can be the collapse of a business or the rejection of being overlooked for a job promotion. A furnace experience can be a health issue, a financial problem, or anything that threatens our peace. We can carry the pain of any furnace experience as long as we want to, or we can let the healer set us free. "And make straight paths for your feet, so that what is lame may not be dislocated *but rather be healed*" (Hebrews 12:13, NKJV; emphasis added).

I live with the memory of January 15, 1997, every day of my life. It was on this day that my first-born daughter went to be with the Lord. It was sudden and unexpected. She was only twenty-five years old and eight months pregnant with our first grandchild. For several years after her death, I would drift away on that day in January. There was no particular place I would go. I just felt I needed to take that day and spend it alone, remembering my daughter. Everyone grieves differently. In 2005, that furnace day was approaching. As I was sitting at my desk thinking about where I was going to spend my day, a soft voice spoke to me in my inner-most being: "When are you going to let me heal you?" There was no scolding tone in the voice I heard. It was soft and loving. After meditating on those words, I remember mumbling, "Today." Leaning back in my chair with my hands raised, I surrendered and received my healing. You have to let your wounds be healed. From that day onward, things have been different. I think about my precious daughter all the time, but my thoughts do not control me emotionally. I do not carry the smell of that furnace.

A Scar Is a Healed Wound

I was notorious for picking at the scab of my wounds when I was growing up. Because of that, my wounds usually took much longer to heal than most. Some of the small cuts I received left bigger scars than they should have because I was always picking at them. Being raised in the country, I spent most of my time outside. We kids were always on some great adventure where we were getting cut, scraped, or bruised in some form or fashion. My mother was constantly saying to me, "Wayne, stop picking at that scab. It will never heal if you don't stop picking at it." My mother was right, but I just could not help myself. Some of my wounds, no matter how minor they may have been, took longer to heal than they should have because of my relentless picking. A wound will never scar until it heals.

This is true of emotional wounds as well. If we keep picking at our emotional wounds, it may take longer for them to heal, leaving bigger scars than they should. "Make straight paths for your feet, so that what is lame may not be dislocated, *but rather be healed*" (Hebrews 12:13, NKJV). We could say it this way, "Let it be healed." In other words, you must give God permission to heal your emotional wounds. That means healing must be intentional. If we choose not to be healed, we can spend the rest of our lives smelling like our divorce, our financial collapse, our broken relationship, our failed business—the list is endless.

One of the biggest lies ever told is, "Time heals all wounds." Not so. I know many people who have taken their emotional wounds to the grave with them. Their epitaphs could read something like this: "They said my emotional hurt and pain would eventually go away, but we have become such good friends. I made the choice to take it with me." It is not wise counsel to tell someone that in time, their emotional pain will go away. We have an enemy who will do everything he can to make sure that we keep picking at our emotional wounds so they do not heal. There is one thing time will do. Time will either vindicate you, or time will indict you. Just give it time.

Internal pain caused by emotional hurt may give the appearance that it will never heal or that it cannot be healed. This is a lie. "[God] heals the brokenhearted and binds up their wounds" (Psalms 147:3, NKJV). These are the words of our heavenly Father, and it is impossible for Him to lie (Hebrews 6:18, NKJV).

If you are battling some emotional trauma right now and are finding it hard to get your emotional life together, I would encourage you to make yourself at home in the words of Jeremiah: "For I know the thoughts that I think toward you, says the Lord, thoughts of peace and not of evil, to give you a future and a hope" (Jeremiah 29:11, NKJV).

The Testimony of Scars

At one time in my life, I played a lot of golf. I still love the game, but I do not have the energy—neither do I want to take the time it takes to play a round of golf. On rare occasions when I do play, it is not uncommon to hear someone who doesn't know me say, "Where did you get those scars on your leg?" I have never heard anyone say, "Where did you get those wounds on your leg?" They do not ask me about wounds because they are healed and have left scars. That's what a scar is. It is a healed wound. We will never have a testimony until our wounds are healed. My scars give me the opportunity to share a little bit of my Vietnam experience and about how Jesus radically transformed my life. A wound does not become a testimony until it heals and becomes a scar.

When Jesus arose from the dead and walked out of the tomb, his disciples were huddled together behind locked doors. They were afraid of the Jewish leaders who had seemingly been successful in crucifying their Lord. All of a sudden, Jesus stepped into the room. The first thing Jesus said to the disciples was, "Peace be with you" (John 20:19, NKJV). Then He showed them his hands and his side. What did they see when Jesus showed them His hands and side? They saw scars. His scars gave testimony to His identity. His wounds were healed. The disciples were overcome with joy when they saw the Lord.

Thomas was not with the other disciples when Jesus appeared to them. When the disciples told Thomas about Jesus appearing to them, he could not believe it. He said, "Unless I see in His hands the print of the nails and put my finger into the print of the nails, and put my hand into His side I will not believe" (John 20:25, NKJV). Pay close attention to what Thomas said. He said he would not believe it was Jesus who had appeared to them unless he saw the scars.

Eight days later, the disciples were gathered together again. This time, Thomas was with them. Even though the doors were shut, suddenly, Jesus stood in their midst again. Jesus focused on Thomas and said, "Reach your finger here, and look at My hands, and reach your hand here, and put it into My side. Do not be unbelieving, but believing" (John 20:27, NKJV). Here is Thomas's response: "My Lord and my God" (John 20:28, NKJV). Thomas knew this was Jesus because of the scars. "By [His] whose stripes you were healed" (1 Peter 2:24, NKJV).

There is no wound or furnace experience that Jesus cannot heal us from, but we must give Him permission. "Let it be healed" (Hebrews 12:13, NKJV). Jesus was hung up for all our hang-ups so we do not have to smell like what we have been through.

If we only knew that we do not have to carry the smell of our furnace experiences.

If We Only Knew
We Can Walk on What
Others Sink In

I COULD HEAR OUR YOUNGEST DAUGHTER RUNNING DOWN THE hallway. She came sliding up to the chair where I was sitting with a big old grin on her face. With excitement in her voice, she said, "Dad, can we walk on water?" Her question took me back a little. I was slow in giving my answer, because I was curious about why she would ask such a question. Then I remembered my message from the previous Sunday: "Walking on what others sink in." I am sure you can guess what it was about: Peter walking on water. Anyway, I responded to her question by asking, "Why do you want to know?" I will never forget her reply. "Because I'm practicing." With that, she ran back down the hallway and jumped back into the bathtub that she had filled with water and continued practicing. I sure admire her faith.

I read an intriguing article about something that I have never had any interest in whatsoever. After reading a few lines, I could not help but finish it. It was a short article about trapeze artists. There is a special relationship between the flier and the catcher on the trapeze. The flier is the one who let's go, and the catcher is the one who catches. The relationship is important. When the flier is swinging high in the air, he or she must let go. Once the flier lets go, he or she must remain as still as possible and wait for the strong hands of the catcher to snatch him or her out of midair. The secret is, the flier must never try to catch the catcher. The flier does nothing but let go. The catcher does everything else. The flier, suspended in midair, must wait in absolute trust. The flier must be still, being confident he or she will be caught by the catcher. The flier must fly, and the catcher must catch. The flier must trust the strong arms of the catcher to be there to catch him or her.

Two statements in this short article are worthy of our attention. The first one is that the flier must never try to catch the catcher. The flier does nothing but let go. The second statement is the one not in control must never try to catch the one in control. It is a recipe for certain disaster if these two instructions are not followed.

You Can't Walk on Water if You Stay in the Boat

Matthew gives us his version of the story about Peter walking on water. "And when Peter had come down out of the boat, *he walked on the water* to go to Jesus" (Matthew 14:29, NKJV; emphasis added). The other disciples had the opportunity to have the same experience but chose to stay in the boat. Most teaching and preaching on this passage deals with Peter's failure, his sinking. To do that is to miss the fact that the man walked on water not once, but twice. Peter was able to walk on what others sink in. I don't think any one of us can relate to walking on water, but we certainly can relate to the sinking part. Maybe it is because of a lack of practice. Is it time for us to fill up our bathtubs with water? Asking for a friend.

When our children are first learning to ride a bike, they have more awkward moments than successes. They may keep their balance for only five feet. The rest of the time, we are helping them balance and move forward. When we share this with family or friends, we say something like, "Oh my goodness, you should have seen my little girl ride her bike today." Or "It was awesome to see my son ride his bike for the first time today." The focus of our story is on the *first five feet* of success they had. We do not mention the other part of the story. They rode their bikes; that is the most important thing. Peter walked on water.

Water Walking

How did the disciples find themselves in the middle of this storm? They had just witnessed a miracle. Not only did they see it with their own eyes, but they participated in it. Bread and fish multiplied in their hands. There was enough food to feed a hungry crowd of five thousand men, not including women and children. It was an all-you-can-eat fish-and-chip meal. This miracle meal came from a boy's lunch of five small loaves of bread and two fish. When the meal was over, Jesus told His disciples to get into their boat and go to the other side of the Sea of Galilee. With their bellies full of fish, they launched out for the other side.

When their boat reached the middle of the sea, a huge storm hit. Matthew said the waves were tossing the boat around and the wind was contrary. Out of nowhere, Jesus appeared. He was walking on the water! That was more disturbing to them than the storm. They thought they were seeing a ghost. To calm their fears, Jesus said, *"Be of good cheer! It is I; do not be afraid"* (Matthew 14:27, NKJV; emphasis added). In response, Peter said, "Lord, if it is You, *command me to come to You on the water*" (Matthew 14:28, NKJV; emphasis added). Jesus said to Peter, *"Come."* Peter stepped out of the boat and began to walk on the very thing that had brought him fear. Jesus put under Peter's feet the very thing that was about to take him under.

Two Important Insights

Two things immediately jump out of this story and beg for attention. The first one is that Peter was walking on the very thing that had been threatening his life. What was first in his face was now under his feet. This is the purpose of this entire book. With the Lord's help, we can walk on what others sink in. If we keep our focus on Jesus, we can walk on the things that keep us emotionally upset. There is one thing for certain: we will never walk on anything if we stay in the boat. Jesus will always extend an invitation for us to step out of the boat.

There is another thing we need to give some attention to. Where we choose to stand will determine how we see things. How we see things will influence what we do. Our positions will always determine our perspectives, and our perspectives will determine our performance. What Peter chose to focus on determined what he was able to do. When he focused on Jesus, he walked by faith on the water. When he focused on the storm (*his situation*), he walked in fear and sank in the water. His focused shifted from Jesus to the situation he had under his feet. His shift in focus moved him from faith to fear.

Fear will sink your boat every time. "For God has not given us a spirit of fear and timidity, but of power, love, and self-discipline" (2 Timothy 1:7, NLT). When this truth becomes a living reality to us, we will be able to walk on what others sink in.

Suspended Between Faith and Fear

Have you ever paid attention to the similarities between these two words: faith and fear? Both believe something is going to happen. Fear believes that what happens will be bad. Faith believes that what happens will be good. Sometimes we can get caught suspended between the two—faith and fear. When this happens, we must fight against the strong impulse to take control of our situations. Remember the article I shared about the trapeze artists? There is only one flier and one catcher. The flier is the one who lets go, and the catcher is the

Wayne Kniffen

one who catches. Once the flier lets go, he or she must remain as still as possible and wait for the strong hands of the catcher. The secret of being successful is that the flier must never try to catch the catcher. The flier does nothing but let go. The catcher does everything. The flier, suspended in midair, must wait in absolute trust. The flier must be still and be confident he or she will be caught by the catcher. The flier must trust the strong arms of the catcher to be there to catch him or her.

Sometimes we can find ourselves suspended between fear and faith. When this happens, our tendency is to take control of the situation, which is the recipe for certain disaster. We need to remain still and wait for the strong hands of the catcher. "Be still and know that I am God" (Psalms 46:10, NKJV).

Jesus took Peter, James, and John, and led them up on a high mountain for some alone time. There on the mountain, Jesus was transfigured before their eyes. These three disciples got a glimpse of His glorious majesty. All of a sudden, there were two men talking with Jesus. One was Elijah, and the other one was Moses. Peter, James, and John recognized these two men, even though millenniums separated them. In his excitement, Peter suggested they build three memorial shelters—one for Jesus, one for Moses, and one for Elijah. Sometimes the best thing to do when you don't know what to say is not to say anything.

"Then a cloud overshadowed them, and a voice from the cloud said, 'This is my dearly loved Son. Listen to Him'" (Mark 9:7, NLT). When the disciples looked around, they saw that Moses and Elijah were gone. As they headed back down the mountain, Jesus told them not to tell anyone what they had seen until He had risen from the grave.

When they got back to where the other disciples were, they saw a large crowd of people surrounding them, and some religious teachers were arguing with them. Jesus asked what all the arguing was about. A man in the crowd spoke up. "Teacher, I brought my son so you could heal him. He is possessed by an evil spirit that won't let him talk. And

52

whenever this spirit seizes him, it throws him violently to the ground. Then he foams at the mouth and grinds his teeth and becomes rigid. So I asked your disciples to cast out the evil spirit, but they couldn't'" (Mark 9:17–18, NLT).

After giving them a brief-but-concise teaching on faithlessness, Jesus told them to bring the boy to him. Jesus asked the boy's dad how long his son had been in this condition. Since he was a little boy, was the dad's answer. Then the dad said to Jesus, "Have mercy on us and help us, if you can" (Mark 9:22, NLT). "What do you mean, 'If I can?' Jesus asked. 'Anything is possible if a person believes'" (Mark 9:23, NLT). The father's response to what Jesus said reveals that he was suspended between faith and fear, between belief and doubt. "I do believe, but help me overcome my unbelief" (Mark 9:24, NLT)! He was like the flier who has turned loose of the trapeze bar; he was suspended between falling and being caught by the catcher. The hardest thing for us to do when we are caught in between is to wait for the catcher: *"Be still and know that I am God"* (Psalms 46:10, NKJV; emphasis added). The word *still* in this verse means to relax. It is difficult to relax when you find yourself dangling in midair, and you are not sure you are going to be caught.

It is hard to sleep when you have a bill that must be paid and you do not have the money to pay it. It is difficult to relax when the biopsy report was not a good one. It is hard to keep going when everything in you is screaming quit. We believe, but we need help with our unbelief. We feel like we are suspended between faith and fear, between belief and unbelief.

The word *know* in this verse speaks of experiential knowledge. It is not about information we have in our heads; it is something that holds us in our innermost being. We can look back on those times when we were in a precarious situation and felt we were going to fall, but just when we thought all hope was lost, we felt the strong hands of the catcher. "If we are unfaithful, he remains faithful, for He cannot deny who He is" (2 Timothy 2:13, NLT). The best thing we can do when we are caught in a challenging situation is turn loose, be still, and wait for the strong hands of the catcher. He can be trusted because He is trustworthy. "See, I have written your name on the palms of my hand" (Isaiah 49:16, NLT).

The Rest of the Story

Wouldn't it be neat if Peter's water-walking story ended with Jesus and Peter walking to the other side of the sea together? When we see that verse 30 begins with *but*, the conjunction of contrast, we know something is about to change. "But when he saw that the wind was boisterous, he was afraid; and beginning to sink he cried out, saying, 'Lord, save me'" (Matthew 14:30, NKJV)! "And immediately Jesus [*the catcher*] stretched out His hand and caught him [*the flier*]" (Matthew 14:31, NKJV). There is only one catcher, and it is not us. The flier does nothing but let go. The catcher does everything. Have you ever found yourself in midair, suspended between fear and faith? Even then, we must wait. We must trust the catcher. The recipe for disaster is for us (the fliers) to try to catch the catcher. *"Be still and know that I am God"* (Psalms 46:10, NKJV; emphasis added).

If we only knew that by faith, we can walk on what others sink in. Trust Him, even when you cannot see or feel Him.

If We Only Knew

Dying Can Teach Us So Much about Living

A WISE, SEASONED PASTOR FRIEND SAID TO ME ONE TIME, "IT IS A shame that dying is the last thing we do, because it can teach us so much about living" (Kirby McGuire). The older I get, the truer those words become. My friend was not talking about being alive. He was talking about living. You can be alive and not be living. When you really live, you can die with precious memories, not with unfilled dreams. Most Christians live so subnormal, that if they ever got normal, they would appear abnormal. If you come into contact with a believer who appears to be abnormal, what does that say about you?

The Dash

On almost every grave marker in a cemetery, there will be two dates under each name. There is a birth date and a death date. This may sound morbid to some, but I love to walk through old cemeteries and read the dates on the headstones. The older the dates, the better.

I stand there in silence and try to imagine what life must have been like for the individual. At one time, the dirt around his or her grave was fresh. The casket of the departed loved one was surrounded by family and friends paying their last respects, sharing memories, and shedding tears. After a heartfelt prayer, the people slowly walked away and continued living their lives. With the passing of time, all those who attended this person's memorial service have each had their own.

About thirty miles west from where I live, there is a ranch that I love to explore. It is like being in another world. There is a butte you can climb, and from the top, you can see all the way to Tucumcari, New Mexico, which is approximately sixty miles away. On top of this butte is a large rock marking the gravesite of a little girl. The year 1865 is crudely but clearly chiseled in the rock. She died while her family was making their way across Texas in a covered wagon. I have stood by that rock several times and allowed my mind to wonder. I cannot imagine how difficult it must have been for this mom and dad. I am sure their tears watered her rocky grave, but the time came when they had to a move on. They had a life to live.

When you look at a grave marker, you will see a small dash between the birth date and the death date. The dash represents the life lived by the person. I think the dash is appropriate because it symbolizes how brief the time is between the two dates. James said that life is like a vapor. We appear for a moment, and then *poof*, we are gone (James 4:14, NKJV). The death of someone we know reminds us of where we are in our dash, especially as we get older and more in touch with our mortality. No matter how long we live, the day will come when people will see a dash between our birth dates and our death dates. Someday, we will hear that someone we know and love has finished his or her dash. We will be saddened, we will grieve, and then we will keep living. One day, my family and friends will hear that I have finished my dash. I certainly want them to remember me, but more importantly, I want them to keep living. I do not want them to waste their dashes. Time is too brief.

Living Our Dash on Purpose

When it comes to living our lives, there are no do-overs. Most of us can look in the rearview mirror of our lives, especially the older we get, and see things we wish we had done differently. Maybe we could have made better choices or made wiser decisions about certain things. There may be things we wish we could change. There is one thing for certain: we cannot go back and change the beginning, but what we can do, is start where we are and change the ending (C. S. Lewis). We can have a good life on purpose. A good life can be lived intentionally.

In July of 1978, Baker Books published *Happiness Is A Choice*, a book written by Frank Minirth and Paul Meier. I remember what my first knee-jerk reaction was when I read the title of that book. I did not believe it. Being happy is not something we can choose. My motivation for reading this book was not to glean information about living a happy life; it was to refute the book's title. Happiness is certainly not a choice. Well, I am here to tell you that it is possible to live a happy life on purpose. Happiness is a choice, and I highly recommend it. I also recommend the book.

The dashes between our birth dates and our death dates is but a moment. A brief one at that. Too many people have not been convinced that it is possible to intentionally live a beautiful and peaceful life. It has nothing to do with the situations we may find ourselves in or the circumstances that may surround us. It would be great if everything in our lives smelled like roses, but roses have thorns. Sometimes the pricks we get from the thorns overpower the beautiful smell of the rose. Jesus told us that as long as we are in this world, we will experience some difficult times. Despite the troubles that come our way, we can be of good cheer and abide in peace (John 16:33, NKJV). This is possible because we abide in Him and He is our peace (Ephesians 2:14, NKJV). Our position in Christ is what makes it possible for us to live our dashes on purpose.

A Future with Hope

If I was given the assignment of branding a scripture on a person's heart, Jeremiah 29:11 may be my scripture of choice. "For I know the plans I have for you, says the Lord. They are plans for good and not for disaster, to give you a future and a hope" (Jeremiah 29:11, NLT). I would encourage you to soak in this verse until it transforms your perspective about life. God is not trying to figure out what He is going to do with and through you. He already knows the plan He has for you, and it is a good plan filled with hope. All you have to do is trust Him.

I remember his big smile as he walked up to me on a Sunday morning with an outstretched hand. After he introduced himself, he said, "I hear you play golf." That was the beginning of a wonderful friendship. Five of us formed our own golfing fraternity. We played a minimum of twice a week and at as many tournaments as we possibly could. Our verbal jabbing each other on the golf course was brutal. It made our bond even stronger.

On one of our men's retreats, my friend accepted Christ as his Lord and Savior. When we got back from the retreat, he shared his testimony in one of our church services. It was an incredible celebration. Our golf outings became even better. During one of our small life-group meetings, I baptized my friend, along with several other guys who had given their lives to Christ as well.

After a few years my friend began to drift. He started missing our golf dates and became less frequent in church attendance. His friendly countenance had been replaced with a vacant stare. I had several visits with him, as did all the guys in our golfing fraternity. Several members of our church family went to see him as well. He continued to drift away. That huge smile he had the first Sunday we met, had disappeared.

A few months later, he moved to another city about a hundred miles south of us. It was not long after that, that his wife came home for lunch one day and found him. He had taken his life by hanging himself. The dashes that separate our birth dates from our death dates are just that—dashes. My friend had lost hope and made the choice to make his dash even shorter.

A future with hope is what God has in mind for His children. We are in this world, and that cannot be denied, but we are not of this world. If we choose to set our affections on things in this world, thinking they will bring us the peace and happiness that we are looking for, we will be sadly disappointed. Happiness is a choice. Can you imagine all the dreams, unwritten books, ideas, inventions, and plans that are buried in our local cemeteries? That is a tragedy that could be avoided. Don't die and have your dreams buried with you. Die with your memories.

Life Is Short, Don't Waste It

A distraught patient phoned her doctor's office. The woman wanted to know if the medication the doctor had prescribed was to be taken for the rest of her life. She was told that it was. There was a moment of silence before the woman continued. "I'm wondering then, just how serious my condition is. This prescription is marked 'no refills!'"

"No refills"—this could be said about living life on this side of eternity. "How do you know what your life will be like tomorrow? Your life is like the morning fog—it is here for a little while, then it is gone" (James 4:14, NLT). Life is like the morning fog: it is brief. This is why there will be a small dash between our day of arrival and our day of departure on our headstones. The days may be long, but the years are short. The best way to get the maximum out of living the abundant life that we were given when we were born from above is to live as if Jesus died yesterday, arose today, and is coming back tomorrow. If we lived life with that kind of mindset, don't you think we would probably make sure that we keep the main thing, the main thing?

We are living in a world today that is full of how-to books: books on how to do this, how to do that. There are books written on how to die. Let me give you some wise counsel: save your money. There is no need to buy a book on how to die because you will do it right the first time. The writer of the book of Hebrews says that each person is destined to die (Hebrews 9:27, NLT). The issue is not about dying; it is about living. But dying can teach us so much about living.

Paul gives us an incredible insight into living and dying in his letter to the believers at Philippi. "For me, *living means living for Christ, and dying is even better. But if I live, I can do more fruitful work for Christ. So I really don't know which is better. I'm torn between two desires: I long to go and be with Christ, which would be far better for me. But for your sakes, it is better that I continue to live"* (Philippians 1:21–24, NLT; emphasis added). Paul says that he is torn; he is unable to decide what is best for him, living or dying. For him to say this and believe it, he has to have an understanding about what living is all about.

This is the Achilles' heel for most believers. We do not know what living life is all about. Busyness has distorted our focus. We have schedules to keep, appointments, doctor visits, school activities, social gatherings, occasional church services, businesses to run, employees to take care of, and our lists continue. Before we know it, our long days have become short years. We could say carpe diem, but we did not seize the day.

To Paul, authentic living is all about Christ. This is why he wrote these words: "When *Christ who is our life* appears, then you also will appear with Him in glory" (Colossians 3:4, NKJV; emphasis added). It is okay to plan and look toward the future, just make sure you include God in your planning. "What you ought to say is, '*If the Lord wants us to,* we will live and do this or that'" (James 4:15, NLTV; emphasis added).

Greet Every Morning with a Prayer Kiss

Before Betty Ann and I got married, we had some deep conversations about how we were raised. It amazed us how similar our stories were. Some of the things we had in common were very good. And there were also some things that we both experienced that were not easy to talk about.

One day, I took her for a ride to see where I grew up. Every house my family lived in when I was growing up was still standing—all but one. The one that was no longer there was either moved or had fallen down, but I am pretty sure it was the latter. At each stop, I would share a childhood memory with her. Of course, some of the stories may have been embellished a little bit.

I also had an ulterior motive for taking her to the country. My plan was to use this outing to steal my first kiss. My scheme unfolded even better than I thought it would. To my utter amazement, there was a store that my family had frequented that was still operational. Of course, she got an earful of my experiences there, especially the green pear that I once threw at a sign. I will leave that story for later.

Here was my plan: I asked Betty Ann if she wanted something to drink. Before I got out of my truck to fetch it, I said, "BA, whatever you do, never trust a cowboy." Of course, she asked why. I told her to lean over and kiss me on the cheek and then I would tell her. When she leaned over to kiss me on the cheek, I turned and faced her. You guessed it, she smacked me right on the lips. Mission accomplished. When I got back in the truck, she looked at me and said, "Smooth move cowboy. Smooth." That was not our last kiss. As husband and wife, we usually met at the coffee maker every morning and greeted each other with a morning kiss. It was not uncommon to hear her say, "Good morning, cowboy."

If we begin each day with a prayer kiss, we will be able to deal with our commitments, problems, priorities, distractions, and obstacles that we may encounter much easier. Living each day as if Christ died yesterday, arose today, and is coming back tomorrow is how we live for Christ.

"For everything there is a season, a time for every activity under heaven. *A time to be born and a time to die*" (Ecclesiastes 3:1–2, NLT; emphasis added). We all have a birth date and a death date assigned to us. We have no say in either. The dashes between these two dates are full of choices. Our days may be long, but our years are short. Let us redeem the time.

If we only knew that dying could teach us so much about living.

9

If We Only Knew
Our Way Out of Temptation

I THINK OSCAR WILDE NAILED THE SUBJECT ON TEMPTATION FOR us when he wrote, "I can resist anything except temptation." Let me give you a few more quotes about temptation that may awaken your interest in this subject:

> "The trouble with resisting temptation is, it may never come your way again" (Korman's Law).

> "I usually avoid temptation unless I can't resist it" (Mae West).

> "Lead me not into temptation; I can find the way myself" (Rita Mae Brown).

> "Opportunity only knocks once, but temptation leans on the doorbell" (Red Symons).

We chuckle at these quotes because temptation is not only familiar to us; it is something we face on a daily basis. Sometimes we are successful in our resisting, and sometimes we fall flat on our faces. This subject immediately triggers some questions: (1.) Is temptation a sin? (2.) Does God ever tempt us to test us? (3.) Was Jesus tempted? (4.) Can God be tempted? (5.) When we are tempted, does it mean we are bad people?

Back in the early 1970s, a man by the name of Louis Bell took me under his wing and began fathering me in the faith. He encouraged me to start internalizing scripture by using the Topical Memory System (TMS) produced by the Navigators. My first assignment was to internalize the five basic assurances for the believer. I can regurgitate them today: (1.) The assurance for forgiveness (1 John 1:9, KJV). (2.) The assurance of answered prayer (John 16:24, KJV). (3.) The assurance for guidance (Proverbs 3:5–6, KJV). (4.) The assurance of salvation (1 John 5:11–12, KJV). (5.) The assurance of victory over temptation (1 Corinthians 10:13, KJV).

I want us to set our crosshairs on number five, the assurance of victory over temptation.

The Anatomy of Temptation

"The temptations in your life *are no different*_[common] from what others experience. And God is faithful. He will not allow the temptations to be more than you can stand. *When* you are tempted, *He will show you a way out*_so you can endure" (1 Corinthians 10:13, NLT; emphasis added).

There are three significant things about temptation that we find in this verse: (1.) All temptations are common to everyone. The enemy will not tempt you with something that no one else has ever faced.(2.) This verse says *when* temptation comes. It is not if temptation comes, it is when it comes. (3.) Because God is faithful, He has already provided a way of escape for us. When we are tempted, He will show us the way out.

James pulls the curtain back and exposes temptation for what it is. "Blessed is the man who endures temptation, for when he has been approved, he will receive the crown of life which the *Lord* has promised to those who love Him. Let no one say when he is tempted, 'I am tempted by God'; for *God cannot be tempted* by evil, *nor does He Himself tempt anyone*" (James 1:12–13, NKJV; emphasis added). That answers questions number two and number five that we began with. God will never test us with temptation, nor can He be tempted. "But each one is tempted when he is drawn away by his own *desires* and *enticed*. Then, when desire has *conceived* it gives *birth* to sin; and sin, when it is full grown, brings forth *death*. Do not be deceived, my brethren" (James 1:14–16, NKJV; emphasis added).

This passage in James reveals the anatomy of temptation for us. Track what James says about temptation. Desire, temptation, conception, birth, death. Temptation comes when we are drawn away by our own desires. The enemy focuses on our desires and uses them to tempt us. A desire is a strong feeling of wanting to have something, or wishing for something to happen. Instead of using the word *desire*, we could use the words *yearning, hankering, wish, want, itch, thirst, impulse,* or *longing*. When our desires begin to pull us away for what is right and good, temptation comes knocking. Temptation is the desire to do something that is unwise or wrong. Some other words we can use for temptation are *lure, seduction, pull, decoy, bait, snare, trap, impulse, urge,* or *inclination*.

All Temptation Is Common to Man

Let's go back and look at the two things that 1 Corinthians 10:13 says about temptation. All temptation is common. That means that you will never be sucker punched with a temptation that no one else has never been tempted with. You will never face a temptation that has been designed just for you. Here is more good news: our faithful heavenly Father has already provided a way of escape from every temptation you will ever face.

"Do not love the world or the things in the world. If anyone loves the world, the love of the Father is not in him. For all that is in the world—*the lust of the flesh, the lust of the eyes, and the pride of life*—is not of the Father but is of the world" (1 John 2:15–16, NKJV; emphasis added). John gives it to us in black and white. Every temptation comes through one, or all three of these gates: the flesh gate, the eye gate, or the pride gate. This is why Paul referred to temptation as *common to man*. Temptation comes through three gates, and three gates only. It will come through the flesh gate, the eye gate, or the pride gate. All we need to do is keep the gates closed.

Our Way of Escape

Paul used the phrase, *It is written* or *For it is written*, many times in the letters he wrote in the New Testament (1 Corinthians 9:9, NKJV). Jesus used these phrases more times than anyone else. "For it is written" (Matthew 4:4–6, NKJV). Why is this so important, or is it? I believe the following passage will give us the answer. "Then some of the itinerant Jewish exorcists took it upon themselves to call the name of the Lord Jesus over those who had evil spirits, saying, 'We exorcise you by the name of Jesus who Paul preaches.' Also, there were seven sons of Sceva, a Jewish chief priest, who did so. And the evil spirit answered and said, *'Jesus I know, and Paul I know; but who are you?'* Then the man in whom the evil spirit was leaped on them, overpowered them, and prevailed against them, so that they fled out of the house naked and wounded" (Acts 19:13–16, NKJV; emphasis added).

In my BC (before Christ) days, I found myself in more fights than I care to remember. The ones that really stand out in my mind are the ones where I came up on the short end. I can honestly say, though, I have never had my clothes beaten off. I find this event in the book of Acts interesting, because Jesus and Paul said, *"For it is written"* more than anyone in the New Testament. They understood the power of the word of God and that the written word of God was their *way of escape*.

The enemy knew who they were. This is why Louis Bell, the man who fathered me in the faith, challenged me to hide the word of God in my heart. It is not if temptation comes, it is when. When temptation comes, our way of escape is to take our stand on the word of God and do what Jesus and Paul did. Declare with great boldness, "For it is written," and then throw the word of God in the face of the enemy.

Jesus Is Our Example

Jesus set the example for us on how to escape temptation. We can win our battle with temptation because He won. Satan came at Jesus with everything he had in his temptation arsenal (Matthew 4:1–11, NKJV). Every time Satan tried to seduce Him, Jesus would say, *"It is written"* (Matthew 4:4–10, NKJV), and then He would quote the word. The enemy was defeated every time with the word of God. Why is the word so effective in our battle with temptation? Because the word of God is truth (John 17:17, NKJV). The devil is a liar, and he does not stand in the truth. When he speaks, he speaks lies. He is a liar and the father of all lies (John 8:44, NKJV). God's word (truth) exposes his lie and becomes our way of escape every time temptation comes knocking.

"Seeing then that we have a great High *Priest* (Jesus) who has passed through the heavens, Jesus, the Son of God, let us hold fast our confession. For we do not have a High Priest who cannot sympathize with our weaknesses, but *was in all points tempted as we are, yet without sin*. Let us therefore come boldly to the throne of grace that we may obtain mercy and find grace to help in time of need" (Hebrews 4:14–16, NKJV; emphasis added). Being tempted is not a sin; neither does it mean we are bad people. Jesus was tempted, yet He did not sin.

The Living Word (Jesus) took His stand on the written word. We can win our battle with temptation every time through the Living Word of God. "For in that He Himself has suffered, being tempted, He is able to aid those who are tempted" (Hebrews 2:18, NKJV).

Let Jesus Answer the Door When Temptation Knocks

In chapter 8 of my book *The Scam*, I deal with the three gates sin knocks on: the flesh gate, the eye gate, and the pride gate. "For all that is in the world—the lust of the flesh, the lust of the eyes, and the pride of life—is not of the Father but is of the world" (1 John 2:16, NKJV). If we know how temptation presents itself, we will be more prepared to keep these gates closed. When the enemy knocks, tell Jesus it is for Him. He will be more than happy to answer the door.

Let me give you a simple definition of temptation. It primarily denotes a trial in which a person has a free choice of being faithful or unfaithful to God. Temptation in and of itself is not sin; it presents us with the opportunity to sin. Even Jesus was tempted, but he did not capitulate. "For we do not have a High Priest who cannot sympathize with our weaknesses, *but was in all points tempted as we are, yet without sin*" (Hebrews 4:15, NKJV; emphasis added). Satan was successful in his attempt to get the first man, Adam, to give in to temptation, but he failed when he tried to get the second man, Jesus, to take the bait (1 Corinthians 15:47, NKJV). Jesus did what Adam and Eve should have done but did not do. When temptation came knocking, Jesus stood on the written word of God, which is truth (John 17:17, NKJV). The written word of God is the enemy's kryptonite because the word of God is truth. Since the devil is a liar, the truth will defeat him every time. He is defenseless against truth. The more of the word of God (truth) you have in you, the more resistant against temptation you will be. "I have hidden your word in my heart, that I might not sin against you" (Psalms 119:11, NLT). This is our way out of temptation. Temptation is inevitable, but temptation is not irresistible.

Satan's Scheme

Here is Satan's scheme: If you thought it, you might as well do it because you are already guilty for thinking it. After all, didn't Jesus say this? "You have heard the commandment that says, 'You must not commit adultery.' *But I say, anyone who even looks at a woman with lust has already committed adultery with her in his heart'*" (Matthew 5:27–28, NLT; italics added). This seems to be indisputable evidence that you are guilty of adultery if you have ever looked at a woman and had lust in your heart.

The law says you must not commit adultery, but Jesus said that if you lust in your heart, you have already committed adultery. When you read this passage of scripture, keep this in mind: Jesus was born under the law (Galatians 4:4, NKJV) and is speaking to people who were under the law. Jesus quotes the law on several occasions in the sermon he gave on the mountainside: "You have heard the commandment." (Matthew 5–7, NKJV). Then He says, "But I say" (Matthew 5–7, NKJV). When Jesus says this, He is taking His listeners beyond the law into the realm of grace. In His teaching on the mountainside (the Sermon on the Mount), Jesus is subtly introducing the new covenant of grace He came to establish. Grace removes you from being under the law and empowers you to live life beyond the law. It is a shift from having to do something (follow the law) to getting to do something (grace). Jesus's Sermon on the Mount is showing the people that they are not living up to what they say they are living under, the law. It is not possible for anyone to live out the commandments of the law because it requires personal, perpetual perfection.

When you accepted and received Jesus as your Lord and Savior, you were given a new heart. "Anyone who belongs to Christ has become a new person. The old life is gone; a new life has begun" (2 Corinthians 5:17, NLT)! Your old life is gone, and that includes your old heart. The new life you have been given has a new heart. Ezekiel wrote about this more than seven hundred years before Jesus was born. "I will give you *a new heart,* and I will put *a new spirit* in you. I will take out your stony, stubborn heart and give you a tender, responsive heart" (Ezekiel 36:26, NLT; emphasis added).

When you had your born-from-above experience with Christ, you were given a completely new life, which includes a new heart—a heart that knows God. As a child of God, your battle with temptation is not a heart issue; it is a flesh issue. The enemy of our souls wants us to believe that our new-creation lives are driven by the heart of our old lives. Most believers are convinced that even though they have been given a new life, this new life still has the old, corrupt heart.

Paul writes extensively about this in the book of Romans. If we set our minds on the flesh, we will live by the flesh (Romans 8:5, NKJV). Notice the words *on* and *by*. As new creations, we are not in the flesh; we are in the spirit. But even though we are in the spirit, we can set our minds on the flesh, and when we do, we find ourselves living by the flesh. Just because we are living by the flesh does not mean we are in the flesh. "But you are not in the flesh but in the Spirit, if indeed the Spirit of God dwells in you. Now if anyone does not have the Spirit of Christ, he is not His" (Romans 8:9, NKJV).

If we only knew that the Lord has guaranteed a way of escape from every temptation that we will ever face in life. We will reign in this life.

10

If We Only Knew

Winning in Our
Thought Lives

IN MY GROWING-UP YEARS, I WAS KNOWN FOR THROWING ROCKS. Country people in East Texas call it *chunking*. I was told time and time again to stop chunking. "You're goin' to break sump'um or put sum'un's eye out," is usually what they told me. Chunking did get me into hot water a few times. I always had my pockets full of ammo: green plumbs, small green pears, tiny peaches, rocks, and more. It really did not matter. All I needed was a projectile.

Then, it happened! A few miles down the blacktop road from our house was a store owned and operated by a man named Ben Smith. It was our equivalent to the modern-day convenience store. They had just about anything you wanted—ice cream, soda, water. At least a six-year-old boy thought so. On occasions, my mother would take us kids with her when she went to shop. On one of those trips, I loaded down the back floorboard of the car with green pears. This was my ammo. When my mother went inside the store, I made a bet with my brother that I could hit the sign that hung between two gas pumps. This was in the day when the gas pumps had the big glass ball on top, and you could see the gasoline inside the pump. I opened the back door of the car and stepped out, locked and loaded, with a small green pear in hand. I wound up, took aim, and let it fly. My trajectory was a little low and a tad off center. Maybe I did not allow for the wind. I did not hit the sign, but I nailed the glass globe on top of the pump—dead center. The smashing of the glass brought every adult inside Ben Smith's store running out the front door. There I stood with both front pockets of my jeans overflowing with small green pears. My mother was eyeballing me with that what-in-the-world-did-you-do look. With hands on her hips, she headed my way. To this day, I have no idea how she knew it was me. Placing her hands on my shoulders, firmly, she said, "What were you thinking?" That was a strange question to ask a six-year-old boy. I knew what I was thinking. I was thinking that I was going to hit that sign, but I missed. That's all I want to share about this story.

Have you ever looked at someone you personally know and wonder, what in the world are they thinking? Maybe we do have a thinking problem. How important is our thought lives? Does it really matter what we think? Thoughts are just thoughts. Well, it does matter. Thoughts have the power to determine destiny. "Plant a thought, reap an action. Plant an action, reap a habit. Plant a habit, reap a character. Plant a character, reap a destiny" (Ralph Waldo Emerson). The fruit of our thoughts are words. Words paint pictures and can lead to actions. Actions that are repeated can become habits. Habits mold and shape character. Character determines destiny. I would say that having a good, healthy thought life is crucial to having a happy life. We are today what we thought yesterday. We will be tomorrow what we think today.

You Must Be at Peace with God to Know the Peace of God

What consumes our minds will ultimately control our lives. This is why it is so important for us to take control of our thought lives. Yes, take control. I realize that unhealthy thoughts can sneak in occasionally. When that happens, it does not mean you are a bad person. The enemy is faithful in living up to his job description and will do everything he possibly can to smuggle unhealthy thoughts into our heads. But we have the power to decide how long they stick around. We cannot stop birds from flying over our heads, but we can keep them from building a nest in our hair. We may not be able to keep bad thoughts from sneaking in occasionally, but we have maximum control over how long they stay. We need to evict them quickly.

In Paul's letter to the Philippians, he talks about the peace of God and the power it has to protect our emotions and our thoughts. "The *peace of God*, which surpasses all understanding, *will guard your hearts and minds* through Christ Jesus" (Philippians 4:7, NKJV; emphasis added). It is impossible to enjoy the *peace of God* if you are not at *peace with God*. "Therefore, having been justified by faith, we have *peace with God* through our Lord Jesus Christ" (Romans 5:1, NKJV; emphasis added). You cannot appropriate something that you do not have access to. A person will never be able to enjoy a peaceful thought life, until he or she has accepted and received Christ as his or her personal Lord and Savior. Christ is our peace (Ephesians 2:14, NKJV).

In the book of Philippians, Paul tells us how to win the battle that goes on between our ears and in our heads (Philippians 4:6–9, NKJV). We will be victorious in our thought lives when we worry about nothing, pray about everything, give thanks in all things, think on the best thing, and then do the right thing.

Worry About No Thing

The first thing Paul says is to worry about nothing. Is that possible? Keep in mind that the word of God would not tell us to do something if it is not possible for us to do. Worry about nothing. The story is told of a guy who was a chronic worrier. He went into the worry mode when he had nothing to worry about. Worrying over the lack of money was his biggest struggle. One day, his friends saw him wearing a big smile, and the look of peace was all over him. Everyone was shocked.

"Why are you so peaceful?" they asked him.

"I hired a professional worrier to do my worrying for me," was his response. When they asked him how he was going to pay the professional worrier, he said, "That is his first worry." We do not have to hire someone to do our worrying for us, because we have Jesus. Worry about nothing.

Pray About Everything

The second thing Paul says is to pray about everything. If this sounds impossible, it is because we do not understand what prayer is. Prayer is not a monologue, where we do all the talking. Prayer is a dialogue. We talk, then we listen. Have you ever had the unpleasant experience of having a one-sided conversation with someone, and you could not get a word in edgewise? Imagine how it must grieve the Holy Spirit when we bombard Him with questions, requests, and petitions, but then we do not allow Him time to answer. I wonder how much wisdom we have walked away from in our prayer time because we did not take the time to listen. Prayer is having a conversation with the one who knows everything about everything and has promised to teach us all things. If we can remember everything we said when we had our prayer time with the Lord, but we cannot recall anything that He said to us, then the question we must ask ourselves is, did we really pray? Prayer is having a conversation with our heavenly Father. In a conversation, both parties have the opportunity to speak. Pray about everything.

Thank Him in All Things

The third thing Paul says is to thank God in all things. Many people shy away from this admonition because they misread what Paul said. He did not say to thank God *for all things*. He said to thank

God *in all things*. Thanking God in the midst of all things, no matter how difficult they may be, is the death blow to the enemy of our thought lives. Being thankful is to be full of thanks. Expressing thanks to the Lord no matter what is going on in our lives stimulates healthy thoughts. Thanksgiving leads to thanks-living. Do not focus on your cup being half full or half empty. Thank Him for giving you a cup. Thank Him in all things.

Think on the Best Things

The fourth thing Paul says is to think on the best things. That means we can intentionally set our minds on things that are healthy, things that are true, honorable, right, pure, lovely, and good—things that are excellent and worthy of praise. These are the things we should mediate on, because we are shaped by our thoughts. We become what we think. *"For as he thinks in his heart so is he"* (Proverbs 23:7, NKJV; italics added). Our future is determined by what we allow to stay in our minds. A wandering mind is the beginning of a wandering life, so think on the best things.

Do the Right Thing

The fifth thing Paul says is to do the right thing. I find it interesting that doing what's right follows thinking right. When our minds are set on healthy things, our inclinations are to live right. Have you ever heard this? "What you're doing speaks so loudly, I can't hear what you're saying" (Ralph Waldo Emerson). When we choose to do right, the peace of God stands guard over our feelings and our thoughts. Do the right thing.

Capturing Our Thoughts

The path to living the abundant life we received when we accepted Christ as our Lord and Savior starts and ends between our ears. We can never overstate the power of the human mind and how our thoughts help shape who we are, how we live, and what we become. "For as he thinks in his heart, so is he" (Proverbs 23:7, NKJV). I love what Mary Kay Ash said about the power and the influence of a person's thoughts. "If you think you can, you can. If you think you can't, you're right." That just about sums it up.

One of the first messages Jesus preached was about the importance of thinking right. "Jesus began to preach and to say, '*Repent*, for the kingdom of heaven is at hand'" (Matthew 4:17, NKJV; emphasis added). Jesus uses the word *repent*, which is the Greek word *metanoeo*, meaning, "to change one's mind." Repentance is not something we do with our mouths; it is about changing the way we think. I have heard countless numbers of people say about their struggles with a particular sin, "I can't get victory over this sin, and I've repented over and over." That is the problem. Repentance is not about being sorry for the wrong we do; it is about changing our minds about what we are doing. When we think about sin the way God thinks about sin, we will not have a problem overcoming a besetting sin. When we think and feel about sin the way the Lord does, victory over sin is assured.

When Paul wrote his second letter to the Corinthian church, he told them they were in a spiritual war, and the way to win this war was to take every thought captive (2 Corinthians 10:5, NKJV). The best way to capture our thoughts is to be still in the presence of God. This may be one of the hardest things for us to do today because we are so busy. "Be still, and know that I am God" (Psalms 46:10, NKJV). Capturing thoughts requires stillness, which most of us don't have time for. We seem to find time to do just about anything we want to do, but we cannot find time to be still in God's presence. Until we do, unhealthy thoughts, emotions, and feelings will continue calling the shots in our lives.

Our reality is shaped by our thought-lives, which are determined by our perceptions, how we choose to see things. Reality is not how we see things. Reality is what God says about things. So, the best way to win in our thought lives is to see life as God sees life. We do that by making our home in His word. "Jesus said to those Jews who believed in Him, 'If you abided [*make your home*] in my word, you are my disciples indeed. And you will know the truth, and the truth shall make you free" (John 8:31–32, NKJV; emphasis added). Knowing truth is what sets us free, and knowing truth comes from living [*abiding*] in the word of God. Truth does not make you free. The truth you know is what makes you free. Truth will always be the truth whether we know it or not or if we are free or not.

When we are willing to change the way we think, we will find the way we live changes too. We do what we do because of the way we think. If you can get a person to think differently, he or she will eventually start living differently. This is why Jesus emphasized the need to change the way we think. "The kingdom of heaven is now at hand" (Matthew 4:17, NKJV). When Jesus arrived on the earth, He brought heaven's government with Him. The rule of heaven is now on the earth. Earthly thinking will not fit into heavenly living. This is the spiritual battle we are fighting today. Even though we are new creations in Christ, we are still thinking like we did before we had our born-from-above experiences. "Do not be conformed to this world, but be transformed by the renewing of your mind, that you may prove what is the good and acceptable and perfect will of God" (Romans 12:2, NKJV). We flesh out our new-creation identities by changing the way we think.

Let me quote the great theologian Winnie the Pooh: "Did you ever stop to think, and forget to start again?" And your answer is?

A Thought Cannot Live unless It Is Spoken

Sometimes a person's greatest accomplishment is keeping his or her mouth shut. I would venture to say that this may be a challenge for most of us. The story is told of a state trooper who pulled a motorist over for speeding. The guy driving the speeding vehicle also had a smart mouth to go along with his heavy foot. On top of this, he was not having a good day. A speeding ticket would add to his frustration.

The immediate exchange between the trooper and this fellow was a little tense, to say the least. The officer was doing everything within his power to keep things civil. As he was handing the frustrated speeder his driver's license back, along with the speeding ticket to sign, the driver said to the trooper, "What would you do if I refused to sign this ticket and called you a numskull?"

The trooper said, "I would probably place you under arrest and take you to jail."

The speeding driver then said, "What if I thought you were a numskull?"

The trooper responded as kindly as he could, "Sir, I can't do anything to you for what you think."

To this, the driver said, "I think you are a numskull, and I am not going to sign this ticket."

I bet you can guess where this speeding driver spent the rest of his day.

I made this story up to make a point. A thought cannot live unless it is spoken. We give life to thoughts by speaking them. The enemy wants us to believe that since we thought it, we might as well say it. Oftentimes, we justify our quick triggers to speak our minds by saying, "I'm just speaking my mind," as if speaking our minds is always a sign of self-confidence and independence. The truth is, many of the thoughts that traffic through our minds are not even ours. They may sound familiar, but they belong to the enemy. When we fall for his trick and speak them aloud, we are speaking his mind and giving life to his thoughts. This is called a familiar spirit. We have heard this voice so often that we are convinced they are our thoughts.

If we are going to give life to our thoughts, let's make sure our thoughts are good, honorable, and healthy. It is wise to make sure the thoughts we give life to by speaking them produce life. Life begets life. We need to constantly ask ourselves, what are we giving life to? Sometimes it is called *the fruit of our lips*. "Therefore by Him let us continually offer the sacrifice of praise to God, that is, *the fruit of our lips*, giving thanks to His name" (Hebrews 13:15, NKJV; emphasis added). "A man will be satisfied with good by *the fruit of his mouth*" (Proverbs 12:14, NKJV; emphasis added).

I was told when I was growing up that a narrow mind and a wide mouth go together. Why teachers would say that to me puzzles me to this day. "Plant a thought, reap an action. Plant an action, reap a habit. Plant a habit, reap a character. Plant a character, reap a destiny" (Ralph Waldo Emerson). The end is determined by the beginning—a thought.

Dr. Caroline Leaf writes in her book *Switch on Your Brain*, "As we think, we change the physical nature of our brain. As we consciously direct our thinking, we can wire out toxic patterns of thinking and replace them with healthy thoughts." Let these words gain traction in your thinking: "As we consciously direct our thinking, we can wire out toxic patterns of thinking and replace them with healthy thoughts." Thinking healthy thoughts is something we must do intentionally.

If we only knew that it is possible to take control of our thought lives.

If We Only Knew
God Is Not Out to Get Us

Is God unapproachable? Is He inaccessible? Is the Lord ever unavailable? Many Christians think so. He is viewed as a distant deity by a lot of religious people. Somehow, we have been convinced that God is really out to get us and that He is hard to please and very stern. If we step out of line too far, we can expect to get whacked over the head. Many parents have said to their children, "God's going to get you if you don't stop that." A seed of fear has been planted in the hearts of children toward God. It is very difficult to love and relax with someone you are afraid of. God is not the ultimate cosmic cop. He is our heavenly Father who is full of love and compassion. He desires nothing but the best for His children. God is not out to get us. He is out to love us.

God is certainly to be revered. He is God. "*The fear of the Lord* is the beginning of knowledge, But fools despise wisdom and instruction" (Proverbs1:7, NKJV; emphasis added). The word *fear* is not an unpleasant emotion caused by a belief that someone or something is dangerous. To fear the Lord is to have a deep sense of respect for Him and to be in awe of who He is. It speaks to our being in submission. Our heavenly Father does not want us to live in terror of Him; He wants us to live in trust.

Our Heavenly Father Is Approachable

The incarnation was a tangible expression of just how much we are loved by our Creator. God literally wrapped Himself up in human flesh and birthed Himself. "And she [Mary] brought forth her firstborn son, and wrapped Him in swaddling clothes, and laid Him in a manger, because there was no room for them in the inn" (Luke 2:7, NKJV; emphasis added). Jesus's birthplace was a low-rise manger, not a high-rise mansion in an affluent neighborhood. This made Him approachable to anyone, no matter his or her rank in society: the up-and-out as well as the down-and-out, and all those in-between, have a standing invitation to approach Him.

In his letter to the church in Rome, Paul talks about the Father's approachability by His children. We are not fearful slaves. When God adopted us, we received His Spirit and became a part of His forever family. His Spirit authenticates us as His children. As His children, we may call Him Abba, Father (Romans 8:14–16, NKJV). The word *abba* is an Aramaic term addressing God in a relationship of personal intimacy. Instead of the word *abba* we would use the term *daddy* or *dad*. To address our heavenly Father as *Dad* is offensive to some people. Now that all my children are grown adults, they do not call me Mr. Kniffen. They call me Dad. It does not offend me at all because it is a term of endearment; it expresses the special relationship that we have.

Jesus said, "*Come to me*, all of you who are weary and carry heavy burdens and *I will give you rest*. Take My yoke upon you, let Me teach you because *I am humble and gentle at heart*, and you will find rest for your souls. For My yoke is easy to bear, and the burden I give you is light" (Matthew 11:28–30, NLT; emphasis added). Our heavenly Father is approachable.

Our Heavenly Father Is Accessible

"So let us *come boldly* to the throne of *our gracious God*. There *we will receive His mercy*, and *we will find grace to help us* when we need it most" (Hebrew 4:16, NLT; emphasis added). To come boldly means to enter His presence with confidence. Our birthright privilege as His children gives us permission not only to come into His presence, but we can come with confidence—no fear. We do not have to ring the doorbell, either. It should not be a surprise to find children in their father's house.

We have a dear friend who drops by our house on a regular basis. Jody is the kind of friend who comes around once in a lifetime, if that often. She will usually knock loudly a couple of times on the back door as she walks in. She will say in a loud voice, "Hello, it's me. Is everyone decent?" We respond by telling her to come on in. By that time, she is already in the kitchen. My wife and I love this. Our friend knows we are accessible, and we love that she feels comfortable and welcome enough to walk into our home as she announces her presence.

That is the heart of our heavenly Father. He is easy to talk to and wants us to be comfortable in His presence. We will always be invited to "come on in." Our heavenly Father is always get-at-able—accessible.

Our Heavenly Father Is Available

"God is our refuge and strength, *a very present help in trouble*" (Psalms 46:1, NKJV; emphasis added). God being a very present help means that He is always available to you. He is available at all times. Has anyone ever asked you, "Are you available for lunch any time this week?" What are they saying? They want to know if there is a day they can get with you to have some one-on-one time. Jesus never turned anyone away who came seeking Him for help. Even some of His prayer times were interrupted by people seeking Him. He made Himself available.

You can wake up in the middle of the night and meet with Him. You may need Him in the heat of the day when things are chaotic. It does not matter if you are alone or in a crowd, He is available because He is a very present help. Time with Him does not require an official invitation. We do not have to stand in line and wait until our number is called. Dressed in our Sunday best is not a requirement. Our heavenly Father is not a distant deity, He is our Abba, our Father, and He is always available.

God Is Madly in Love with You

If Christians could ever get ahold of the truth that God is not mad at them, it would radically transform their entire world. God is not mad at you, beloved. He is madly in love with you. This is hard for so many believers to wrap their heads around. How can God love me when I have thoughts like I do, or when I say and do things that I know are not right? Our concept of being loved by God is based on what we do or do not do. Being loved unconditionally by God has nothing to do with what we do; it is about what He has done. Once we get a revelation of what He has done for us, it will change what we do.

"But *God demonstrates His own* love toward us, in that *while we were still sinners Christ died for us*" (Romans 5:8, NKJV; emphasis added). If you struggle with believing that God loves you, soak in this verse until its truth penetrates your doubt and unbelief. God doesn't just say that He loves you; He demonstrated His love by allowing His Son to die for you when you did not want anything to do with Him. While you were still in your sinning state, God proved His love for you by sending His Son to die on a cross in your place. You talk about a gamble! Loving someone who does not love you back is not an easy assignment.

John 3:16 (NKJV) is a verse that most Christians can quote or at least mumble their way through. "For God *so loved* the world …" The intensity of God's love is expressed in this verse. He doesn't just love you, He *"so loves"* you. The object of His intense love is the world. The world is made up of good people and people that are, well, you know. His intense love is for all, no matter the depth of their depravity. God's intense love for all of humankind is not just talk, He demonstrated it. *"He gave His only begotten Son."* That, my friend, is beyond our ability to comprehend. It is to be embraced and accepted. This verse also gives us the reason behind God's love for us. By believing in Him, we are given lives that are everlasting, lives that will never end.

As I was walking down the hallway toward the front offices at church, I heard a lady screaming at her children at the top of her lungs. "God is going to get you if you don't start behaving yourselves!" When she saw me, she had the look of a child who had been caught with his or her hand in the cookie jar. She quickly ushered her children out the side door. I did not want to say anything to her in front of her children, so I waited until the next morning. We had a good, long talk about that moment she had with her children. I shared with this young mother how important it is for a child to grow up knowing that God loves him or her unconditionally. Children need to learn early on that God is a good Father. He is not out to get them. When we discover how much He loves us, we cannot help but love Him back. "We love Him because He first loved us" (1 John 4:19, NKJV).

Many people grow up thinking that God is out to get them. Where did they learn this? From parents and Sunday school teachers who have told them what I heard this lady say to her children. If you step out of line, God will get you. It is being said from pulpits every Sunday in churches all over the world. People hear it expressed in various shapes and forms in bible study groups. A large percentage of believers today see God as a spiritual policeman who is always on patrol looking for spiritual violators. Not only will God get you, but He gets some sort of twisted pleasure out of getting you.

When I first entered the ministry almost fifty years ago, clapping hands in most church services was a sign of irreverence. You certainly never whistled or shouted. That was taboo. In some churches, even responding with an appropriate amen was frowned upon. Many children received spankings for running inside the building. It was not uncommon to hear an adult say to a child or teenager, "Be quiet. This is God's house." This leaves the impression, especially with the young, that the church building where people gather for worship is a quiet zone; it is where God lives, and you certainly do not want to do anything that will disturb Him, because He is grouchy and He just might clean your clock if you are not on your best behavior. And we wonder why there is a big exodus from the church by young adults. We did not lose them when they become young adults. We lost them when they were children, and they left when they become young adults.

The unadulterated truth is, God is madly in love with you. He is not out to get you, no matter what you have been taught or think. "Beloved, let us love one another, *for love is of God*, and everyone who loves is born of God and knows God. He who does not love does not know God, *for God is love*" (1 John 4:7–8, NKJV; emphasis added). Since God is love, He loves you! That should make you shout, whistle, clap, say amen, and dance. Go ahead. You have heaven's permission.

If people understood how much God loved them, they would be running to Him, not from Him. The scripture says that it is the goodness of God that leads to repentance (Romans 2:4, NKJV). God's goodness is what changes the way we think. Always keep this in mind: Whatever God is, He is completely. Since He is good, He is completely good.

The greatest struggle and fear that I see in people is their uncertainty of God's love for them. How can a perfect God love an imperfect person? Many are convinced that they will be turned away by God if they come to Him in a spirit of repentance. After all, they have done it before and did not live up to the bargain they made with Him the last time. Have you ever said, "Lord, you get me out of this and I will ...."? You can fill in the blank. Most of us have written checks with our mouths that our lives did not cash. When the Lord gets us out of our difficult situations, we move on with our lives as if we never wrote a check. How many second chances has the Lord given to us? God is an all-knowing God. He remembers all of those unfulfilled checks we have written to Him, yet He is still madly in love with us. How can we not love a Father like that?

In my growing-up years, I was a mischievous young man. I am cutting myself a lot of slack by my choice of words. To be honest, I was an unruly lad, and it landed me in hot water more often than I want to remember. There is no telling how many times I told God, "If you'll get me out of this, I will be your guy. You can count on me." You see, I knew a lot about God, but I did not know God. I was using Him like a poker chip. When I got on the other side of my trouble, I went on my way like I was in control. If God was not good and if He was out to get me, I would have been fried years ago.

Then it happened! It was in 1968, and the hot water that I found myself in was Vietnam. This was the moment I would make my transition from knowing about God to knowing Him. The cry of my heart that night was not for Him to take me out of my situation—I wanted Him. I was tired of running. My rebellious life had left me exhausted. I was not writing another check with insufficient funds. What was so amazing about this moment was that He did not turn me away. There was no lecture, no reminding me of all the checks that I had written in the past. I never heard, "I told you so. I knew you would come crawling back to me someday." A holy God made Himself available, approachable, and accessible to an ungodly young man.

Not only did the Lord save me that night; He called me to preach the gospel of good news. You talk about a gamble on His part. It has been almost fifty years since I began preaching, and there is only one thing I would do differently if I could do it over. I would start much earlier.

God is not waiting to love a new version of you. He loves you! I guess, in a sense, God is out to get you. He wants you to be a part of His forever family.

If we only knew just how much God loves us. God is available for you. God is approachable by you. God is accessible to you.

If We Only Knew

You Have a Miracle in Your Hands

WHAT DO YOU HAVE IN YOUR HAND? YOUR RESPONSE MIGHT BE, I have a cup of coffee, my bible, my cell phone, or actually, I have nothing. Let me ask this question another way. What are you holding on to? Is there anything you need to let go of but are finding it impossible to release?

Let me tell you up front what you have in your hand. You have a miracle. That's right, a miracle. God is waiting for you to release whatever you may be holding on to, so He can do with it what only He can do—a miracle. Whatever you release will be transformed and given back to you so you can use it to bring honor and glory to God.

Moses: The "Will-Not" Man

In Exodus 3–4, God is having a conversation with Moses, a man who is in his eightieth year of life, about a mission assignment. Are you kidding me? Moses is too old to be used by God—or is he? In this conversation, God told Moses that he had been chosen to deliver His people from Egyptian bondage. Put yourself in Moses's sandals. You are talking to God, who has appeared to you in a burning bush. God tells you that you have been chosen to lead His people out of Egyptian captivity. That's right: God is talking to you through a bush that is on fire. Oh, and you are eighty years old. Maybe now we can understand why Moses said what he said. "I am not your man" (Exodus 3:11, NKJV). "I cannot be your man" (Exodus 4:10, NKJV). "I will not be your man" (Exodus 4:13, NKJV). I am not, I cannot, and I will not. Let me remind you of something just in case you think you can duke it out with God: there is a name for an individual who wants to go toe to toe with God—victim.

Moses could not say yes to God because he still remembered what put him on the backside of the desert; for forty years, I might add. It was hard for him to let that go. Moses had fled to the land of Midian in fear for his life. Here is a little geography tidbit that might interest you. The land of Midian is on the back side of the backside of the wilderness. Moses had given that *delivering the people* business a shot, and look where it had gotten him. And God is asking him to do it again!

Let me give you a brief glimpse in to Moses's life up to this point. He spent the first forty years of his life in Pharaoh's house, learning how to be somebody. Then he spent forty years of his life on the back side of the desert, learning how to be a nobody. Now he was being given the opportunity to see how God could take a nobody and make him a somebody. Let me add a footnote here: all at the age of eighty. I feel I need to keep pointing this out in case someone thinks that doing great things for God is reserved only for the young.

Releasing and Letting Go

God asked Moses, "What is in your hand?" (Exodus 4:2, NKJV). What was Moses holding on to? Moses responded, "It is a rod, it is a stick." God told Moses to cast it down, and when he did, the stick became a serpent. The text says that Moses fled. Fleeing from the snake was the only smart thing Moses did.

When did the stick become a snake? When did the miracle of the stick turning into a serpent happen? When Moses released it and let it go. God then told Moses to reach out and pick the serpent up by its tail. "Moses reached out his hand and caught it, and it became a rod in his hand" (Exodus 4:4, NKJV). The stick that became a serpent was back in the hands of Moses, and it was a stick again. God then told Moses, "And you shall take this rod [*stick*] in your hand with which you shall do the signs" (Exodus 4:17, NKJV; emphasis added). Moses had a miracle in his hands. "And Moses took the rod of God in his hand" (Exodus 4:20, NKJV). The stick was called the rod of God, but it was in the hands of Moses. This is the same rod that Moses lifted up toward heaven and then the waters of the Red Sea parted. It was with this rod that Moses struck a rock and lifegiving water flowed out, quenching the thirst of two to three million people (1 Corinthians 10:4, NKJV). This was truly the rod of God, and notice where it was: it was in the hands of Moses.

Truth We Learn from Releasing

We will never really have what we have not released. It can be your business, a child, your children, grandkids, spouse, marriage, your life, memories, relationships, or whatever. It is a blank check. You fill it in.

I remember a few years ago the excitement that was beginning to gain traction concerning our fiftieth high school graduation celebration. That special day was drawing near. Since my high school days, I have had the unique opportunity to stay in contact with many of my former classmates. It has been a joy and an honor to pray for many of them and to have them pray for me.

As our big celebration day was approaching, several former classmates told me they would not be attending. When I asked why, it did not take long for some of them to tell me the reason they would not be coming. I listened to them vent hurts that went all the way back to our junior high days. Most of their hurts did not come from actual events. The pain they were holding on to came from their perceptions of these events. Their perceptions had become their realities, and they just could not let it go. As long as we choose to hold on to hurts and pains, we cannot experience a miracle of emotional healing. Many people are walking around with wounds that should be scars by now. A scar is a healed wound. An emotional wound will not heal until it is released. Once it is released, God can miraculously heal it, and then that scar becomes a testimony to the goodness of God.

A miracle can happen only when we release whatever we are holding on to. Let's go back to the story of Moses. Even though the Hebrew people were slaves in Egypt, they kept increasing in number. One day, it dawned on Pharaoh that if a foreign enemy ever attacked, the Hebrew people might rise up and join the invading forces and defeat the Egyptians. Here was Pharaoh's plan. He called in the midwives and gave them instructions. When a Hebrew woman was giving birth and it was a boy, they were to kill the baby. If it was a girl, she could live. The midwives feared God more than they feared Pharaoh and refused to carry out the king's command. The king called in the midwives and asked them why they had not carried out his orders. They lied and told him that the Hebrew women were not like the Egyptian women. They were strong. They told the king that by the time they got there, the Hebrew women had already given birth. God dealt with the midwives with favor (Exodus 1:15–22, NKJV).

The king issued another order. Every son that was born was to be thrown into the river and drowned. During this time frame, a baby boy was born to Amram and Jochebed. They named him Moses. Jochebed hid baby Moses as long as she possibly could. *"When she could no longer hide him, she took an ark of bulrushes for him, daubed it with asphalt and pitch, put the child in it, and laid it in the reeds by the rivers bank"* (Exodus 2:3, NKJV; emphasis added).

I cannot begin to imagine what must have gone through this mother's soul when she set her baby adrift in the river. The pain that she must have felt in her heart as she removed her loving hands from that little basket where her baby boy lay, must have been unbearable. Releasing is not easy, but if she had not released Moses, the chances are very good that he would have died with the other babies. I think it is only fitting that we give Jochebed some of the credit for the Israelites' deliverance.

A miracle can happen only when we release whatever we are holding on to. In the same way that Moses turned loose of the stick that was in his hands, when Jochebed released baby Moses, God went to work. It just so happened that Pharaoh's daughter came down to the river to bathe. Her maid servant was with her. When Pharaoh's daughter saw the baby, she sent her maid servant into the river to retrieve him. Guess who was watching? Miriam, the sister of the baby. Do you think that maybe Jochebed had posted Moses's older sister at the river bank to keep an eye on her little brother? Miriam said to Pharaoh's daughter, "Shall I go and get a nurse for you?" Pharaoh's daughter said yes. Well, guess who she got? You guessed it, didn't you? Miriam brought Jochebed, the mother of the baby, to nurse and take care of him. Not only did Jochebed get to raise her baby, but she was paid wagers to do so (Exodus 2:9, NKJV). I would say that was a miracle. This is a beautiful picture of Psalms 23, *"He prepares a table before me in the presence of mine enemies"* (Psalms 23:5, NKJV; italics added). Jochebed raised her son, Moses, in the enemy's house, and the enemy paid her wages to do so. God prepared her a table in the presence of her enemy. How good is our God?

Releasing is difficult because it involves trust. God is trustworthy, but God cannot trust us with what we have not released. There is no age limit when it comes to releasing, either. But the older we get, the tighter we seem to hold on to things. Have I mentioned that Moses was eighty years old when God told him to turn loose of the rod that was in his hand? What are you holding on to?

Releasing and Letting Things Go Is a Heart Issue

If God can trust your heart, He will trust your hands. A heart that cannot be trusted will be very reluctant when it comes to releasing things. How many times have you heard someone say, "If I ever win the lottery, I will make sure my church never has a need"? What makes a person think he or she will be faithful with a lot when he or she cannot be trusted with a little? It is always easier to be generous with something you do not have. "For out of the abundance of the heart the mouth speaks" (Luke 6:45, NKJV). Releasing and letting things go is a heart issue.

Why couldn't Moses say yes to God? Because he was still holding on to the pain and hurt he had experienced forty years earlier. Moses had tried to deliver his people from their Egyptian bondage, and look where it had gotten him: forty years on the back side of the backside of the Midian wilderness. His own people had rejected him because they misunderstood what he was trying to do for them. "[Moses] ... thought his brethren would have understood that God would deliver them by his hand, *but they did not understand*" (Acts 7:25, NKJV; emphasis added). It can be emotionally devastating when you do something that you think is right and then be judged wrong by those you love. After forty years, Moses was still carrying the wounds of that rejection and the emotional hurt caused by his own people's misunderstanding of what he was trying to do for them.

The book of Acts gives us some insight into the emotional struggle the self-exiled Moses had a hard time overcoming. The story is found in Acts 7:22–36 (NKJV). The first thing Luke says about Moses is, "He was mighty in words and deeds" (Acts 7:23, NKJV). How did Moses get so educated, so informed? Being raised in the house of Pharaoh, he had access to the best of the best. Moses was educated in all the wisdom of Egypt.

Even though Moses was physically separated from his own people, his thoughts and heart was always with them. One day, Moses decided to visit the children of Israel. "Now when he was forty years old, *it came into his heart* to visit his brethren, the children of Israel" (Acts 7:23, NKJV; emphasis added). Luke tells us that this decision to visit his people was Moses's idea. This was not a God assignment. It was something he decided to do on his own. Instead of waiting on God, Moses took matters in his own hands. The first thing he saw when he arrived was an Egyptian abusing one of his brethren. Moses stepped in to defend his brother and killed the Egyptian. This was when things started going south for Moses. He was convinced that his people would understand that God was using him to deliver them, but they did not. The next day, he saw two of his brethren fighting. When he tried to break them up, one of the men shouted, "Who made you a ruler and a judge over us? *Do you want to kill me as you did the Egyptian yesterday?*" (Acts 7:28–28, NKJV; emphasis added).

Moses put his running sandals on and fled to the wilderness, carrying all his rejection, emotional pain, and hurt with him. The Midian desert became his home for the next 480 months. Forty years is a long time to live with the hurts, pain, and wounds of one's past. Choosing to hang on to emotional wounds instead of releasing them will prolong one's wilderness experience.

It was just another hot day in the wilderness when Moses saw a bush that was on fire, but it wasn't being consumed. As he went to take a closer look at this incredible sight, the voice of God spoke to him. "I am the God of your fathers—the God of Abraham, the God of Isaac, and the God of Jacob." And Moses trembled and dared not look. Then the Lord said to him, 'Take your sandals off your feet, for the place where you stand is holy ground'" (Acts 7:32–33, NKJV). I find it interesting that the first thing God told Moses to do was to take off his running sandals. His running days were over. God was going to give Moses another shot at the delivering-the-people ministry, this time, with His blessings and guidance.

Our pasts, no matter how long, how difficult, and how painful it may have been, can prepare us for a glorious present and a victorious future. Think about this: The forty years Moses spent in the wilderness learning how to be a nobody prepared and taught him how to lead

God's people in the wilderness—for how long? Forty years. Nothing is wasted with God.

When Moses graduated from the University of Egypt, he was known as a man mighty in words and deeds (Acts 7:22, NKJV). When he graduated from the University of Hard Knocks, he was known as a man of signs and wonders. "He brought them out, after he had shown *wonders and signs* in the land of Egypt, and in the Red Sea, and in the wilderness forty years" (Acts 7:36, NKJV; emphasis added). Why settle for mighty words and deeds when you can experience signs and wonders?

If we only knew that we have a miracle in our hands.

If We Only Knew
All We Need Is a Sling and a Stone

WHEN WE WERE YOUNG BOYS, MY BROTHER, KEITH, AND I WERE taught how to make a slingshot by cutting the tongue out of an old leather shoe. We would then attach a string to each side of the cut-out tongue. Then we would place a rock in the fold of the shoe tongue and twirl it around our heads. When we were ready to send our projectile forward, we would turn one of the strings loose, and the rock would go flying. Without turning one of the strings loose, the rock will not release. You would wear yourself out twirling the sling around your head, accomplishing nothing. It was a lot of fun, and it is amazing how accurate you can get with practice. I will have to confess that many of our practice sessions got us into hot water.

Analogies of the Sling and the Stone

When facing giants, all a child of God needs is *a sling* and *a stone*. The sling is what moves the stone. The sling can represent faith.

"Without faith it's impossible to please God" (Hebrews 11:6, NKJV; italics added). This verse does not say that without faith, it is difficult to please God; it says it is impossible to please God without faith.

The stone can represent Christ. "Therefore, to you who believe, He is precious; but to those who are disobedient, *the stone* which the builders rejected has become the *chief cornerstone,* and a *stone* of stumbling and *a rock of offense*" (1 Peter 2:7–8, NKJV; emphasis added).

In keeping with this analogy, the stone is waiting on the sling. The sling moves the stone. In other words, heaven is waiting on us. Contrary to popular belief, prayer does not move God. Fasting does not move God. Good works do not move God. Giving does not move God. Faith moves God.

A Boy Faces a Giant

David was a sixteen-year-old boy facing off with a seasoned champion. His choice of weapon was a sling and five smooth stones. Armed with faith, this young boy was willing to do what grown men refused to do—face the giant. The men of Israel were saying that Goliath was too big to hit. David was thinking, *He is too big to miss.* Our perspective, how we see things, determines what we are willing to face.

To say David's opponent was a grown man would be an understatement. Goliath was not referred to as a giant for no reason. He was nine feet tall. The armor he wore on his chest weighed 125 pounds. His chest armor probably weighed more than David. We are told that the staff of his spear was like a beam. The tip of it weighed fifteen pounds. Can you imagine the strength it took to throw that thing? In front of Goliath stood an armor barrier holding a shield. If you knew nothing about this story, who would you place your money on, this sixteen-year-old shepherd boy with a sling and a stone, or this beast of a man armed to the teeth? It depends on how you see things.

How you see things will be determined by your position, what seat you have chosen to sit in. The men of Israel were focused on how big their problem was. David was focused on how big his God is.

David was not looking at Goliath through his natural eyes. If he had, it would have been his battle, and he probably never would have taken on the giant. Instead, he chose to look at Goliath through his spiritual eyes. This made it God's battle. David was about to bring the unseen realm into the seen realm, the spiritual realm into the natural realm. What could not be seen was about to be brought into what could be seen. This was done by faith. The sling moved the stone like faith moves God.

Position Determines Our Perspective

If I placed the number six on the floor and stood two individuals, one on each side of the number, and then ask them what they see, I would get two answers. One would say he or she sees a six; the other one would say he or she sees a nine. What determines what they see? Their position. Where we choose to sit or stand will determine how we see things. We have been given free will, so we can choose our position. Our choice of position will determine our perspectives on how we see things. Our perspectives will determine our performances when we are facing giants. Our giants will be too big to hit, or our giants will be too big to miss.

When we have a *giant showdown moment*, our positions will be one of fear or one of faith. Both fear and faith believe something is going to happen. One is bad; one is good. The men of Israel were full of fear and felt there was no way they could take on Goliath. David was full of faith, and he believed he would take out Goliath. How they saw things determined what they believed. What they believed determined what they were able to do.

The same is true with us when we are facing life challenges. It is not *if* we face giants, it is *when*. Our giants can be financial, health issues, marriage, relationships, business, or anything that appears overwhelming. How we perform when that happens will be determined by our perspectives, and our perspectives will be determined by the positions we choose to view our challenges from.

Two Ways of Looking at Giants

There are two ways we can look at the giants we will face in life. Being victorious or going down in defeat will be decided by how we choose to look at our giants.

I have a little exercise that I do on a regular basis that helps me keep things in perspective. It is simple but effective. As I share this information, my suggestion is that you take a pen and a piece of paper and do this exercise as you continue reading.

Draw a horizontal line on the paper. Everything above the line is spiritual. Everything below the line is natural. Go ahead and write that on the graph you have started. This is how God sees things. Things are either natural or they are spiritual (1 Corinthians 2:14–16, NKJV). This will help you to understand how David was able to not only have the courage to take on Goliath, but how he was able to take him out. We will be able to take out our giants the way David did when we begin to see things the way David saw things.

Back to the horizontal line. Everything above the line is the unseen realm; everything below the line is the seen realm. Our identities as believers are determined above the line, in the unseen spiritual realm. There are two expressions that are repeated over and over in the New Testament, describing our identities as believers: *"Christ in you"* (2 Corinthians 13:5, NKJV) and *"you in Christ"* (2 Corinthians 5:17, NKJV). On the chart that you are making, write, *"Me in Christ"* above the line; then write *"Christ in me"* below the line. In John's letter to a cluster of churches made up of both Gentiles and Jews, he addresses their new-creation identities. "Love has been perfected among us in this: that we may have boldness in the day of judgment; because *as He is, so are we in this world*" (1 John 4:17, NKJV; emphasis added). Focus on the last nine words of this verse: "As He is, so are we in this world." When will we be like Christ? This verse says that we are like Christ right now, in this world, which is below the line. Where is Christ at this moment? Ephesians tells us that He is seated at the right hand of the Father. Where are we? Ephesians gives us the answer to that question. "And raised us up together, and *made us sit together in the heavenly places in Christ Jesus*" (Ephesians 2:6, NKJV; emphasis added).

Again, the purpose of this graph you are making is to help you understand your identity in Christ. When you begin to see who you are in Christ, it will change your perspective. Your perspective will empower your performance. You will become a giant slayer.

Before we move on, let's slow-walk our way back through what we have just covered. As believers, we are seated in Christ above the line in the spiritual, unseen realm. At the same time, we are living in the natural seen realm below the line. This is why Jesus said that even though we are in the world (below the line), we are not of the world (above the line) (John 17:15–16, NKJV).

Everything above the line is complete, while everything below the line is being made complete. As believers, below the line, we are becoming what we already are above the line. Since everything above the line, in the spiritual unseen realm, is already complete, that makes the unseen realm more real than the seen realm. You should write that on your graph. I have been made complete above the line. I am being made complete below the line.

Let me keep hammering on this spiritual nail because this is what we hang our new-creation identities on. Colossians 2:10 (NKJV) says that we are complete in Christ; yet Philippians 1:6 (NKJV) says that we are being made complete. Are we complete, or are we being made complete? Maybe we have a contradiction here. Here is something we need to keep in mind: When there appears to be a contradiction in the scriptures, that is exactly what we have, an appearance. Colossians 2:10 (NKJV) is talking about who we are in

Christ above the line. We are complete. Philippians 1:6 (NKJV) is talking about who we are becoming in Christ below the line. Below the line, in the natural realm, we are becoming what we already are in the spiritual realm, above the line. We are in Christ above the line, which makes us complete. Christ is in us below the line, and He is making us complete.

The unseen is more real than the seen. "By faith we understand that the worlds were framed by the word of God, so that *the things which are seen were not made of things which are visible*" (Hebrews11:3, NKJV; emphasis added). Since the things we can see were not made out of things we can see, then the things we can see were made out of things we cannot see. That makes the unseen realm more real than the seen realm. The spiritual is more real than the natural. Life above the line is a believer's reality. We are spiritual beings who have souls and we live in bodies. We are not bodies that have a spirit. As spiritual beings, we are having a temporary physical experience. We are not physical beings having a temporary spiritual experience. As believers, we are in the unseen spiritual realm *in Christ*. Christ is *in us* in the natural seen realm.

God Finishes Something Before He Starts It

There is a passage in the book of Isaiah that blows my mind. "For I am God, and there is none like Me. *Declaring the end for the beginning*" (Isaiah 46:9–10, NKJV; emphasis added). Do you have any idea why God would say there is no one like Him? How many people do you know, who have the ability to finish something before they start it? I am a happy camper when I finish something I start. Before God starts something, He finishes it first.

God demonstrated this unique ability in Genesis 1 when He spoke things into existence. When we want a tree, what do we do? We plant a seed, cultivated it, and, in time, it will mature into what we wanted. What did God do? He spoke a mature tree into existence that had seeds and would bear after its kind. The mature, complete tree was finished before the seed ever existed. The mature tree is the fruit of the root. The fruit (tree) came before the root (seed). This pattern is seen all through the Scriptures. "Even *before He made the world*, God loved us and *chose us in Christ* to be holy and without fault in His eyes" (Ephesians 1:4, NLTV; emphasis added). In Revelation 13:8, we are told that the Lamb was slain before the world was ever made.

This is what we read earlier in Hebrews 11:3. Everything we can see with our physical sight, came from the unseen realm, which makes the unseen more real than the seen. As believers, our identities do not come from our behaviors below the line. Our identities come from our births above the line. We were born from above (John 3:3, NKJV). When we are born again, we are still in this world, but we are not of this world.

Faith Is the Currency of Exchange

In almost every place I have travel to around the world, I've had to exchange my American currency for the currency of the country I am visiting. For me to enjoy the goods and services that country has to offer, this exchange is necessary. In most places, it is mandatory.

We may be citizens of a particular country on this planet, but as believers, we are citizens of the kingdom of heaven too. "For *our citizenship is in heaven*, from which we also eagerly wait for the Savior the Lord Jesus Christ" (Philippians 3:20, NKJV; emphasis added). As kingdom citizens, we have access to the goods and services this kingdom has to offer, but it takes currency. The currency that makes it possible for us to appropriate what is available to us in the unseen realm (spiritual) is faith. We cannot take what is below the line (physical) into what is above the line (spiritual), but we can bring what is in the unseen realm into the seen realm. This is done with the currency of faith.

David Ran to What the Men of Israel Ran From

This brings us back to the sling and a stone. David was able to do what the men of Israel could not do. It was his focus that made the difference. The men were looking at Goliath and were full of fear. David was looking at his God and was full of faith. Both believed something was going to happen.

I can hear David shouting something like this as he ran toward Goliath: "I come to you in the name of the Lord. Today the Lord will conquer you. For the battle is the Lords. He will give you into our hands" (This is my personal paraphrase of 1 Samuel 17:45–47, NKJV). I love these words, "So *David prevailed* over the Philistine *with a sling and a stone*" (1 Samuel 17:50, NKJV; emphasis added).

David was unmoved by the overwhelming odds he faced in the natural realm because he chose to access the spiritual realm with his currency of faith. The position David chose allowed him to have a perspective that empowered his performance. He took the giant out. The impossible became Him-possible.

"And I will give you the keys of the kingdom of heaven, and whatever you bind on earth [natural seen realm] *will be bound in heaven* [spiritual unseen realm], *and whatever you loose on earth* [natural, seen realm] *will be loosed in heaven* [spiritual, unseen realm]" (Mathew 16:19–20, NKJV; emphasis added).

It is time we start appropriating what is rightfully ours in Christ, so the natural realm can see the spiritual realm: on earth as it is in heaven.

If we only knew that all it takes to slay a giant is a sling and the stone.

If We Only Knew

We Can Share Our Father's Home but Not Share His Heart

In Luke 15, Jesus tells a story about a father and his two sons. The younger of the two sons proved to be the most irresponsible. In his devil-may-care attitude, he heads out for the lights and sounds of the big city. He felt it was time to stretch his wings and fly solo. Throwing all caution to the wind, he left the security of his father's home. It was time for him to be his own boss, his own man. He needed to find himself. There was one thing he never considered: he was not going to like what he found.

The oldest son stayed home with his father and kept his nose to the grind. He continued to work, and work hard. For a long time, my sympathy was with the elder son. How could you not feel empathy for him? He remained faithful, shouldered his responsibilities, and did what his younger brother should have done. His father needed him, so he stayed home. When telling this story, the younger son, the one who rebelled and left home, seems to get most of the ink. What we may have overlooked is that the eldest son did stay home physically, but his heart had left, probably long before his younger brother did. He shared his father's home, but he did not share his father's heart.

It was not until his younger brother came home that we actually got to know the older son. Up until the prodigal son's return, we only knew him as the eldest of the two sons.

The Heart of the Eldest Son Is Revealed

How long does it take to kill and prepare a calf for a party? Several hours had to have gone by, yet no one went to the field to tell the eldest son his brother had come home and that his father was throwing a party to celebrate the occasion. Maybe it was because everyone knew him. This would not be the kind of news the eldest son would enjoy hearing, so everyone left him alone. He would find out soon enough.

When his daily chores were done, the elder son headed for the house. Another hard day's work was in the books. It was time to clean up and get ready for the evening meal. Tomorrow, he would start over again. As he drew near the house, he could hear the music and the dancing that was coming from the celebration. He had no idea what the special occasion was all about. He had been left in the dark—again.

When he asked what was going on, one of the servants told him that his brother had come home and his father was so thrilled to have him back safe and sound, he threw a party. The elder son's response to this news tells us why no one went to the field to let him know his brother had come home. *"He was angry and would not go in"* (Luke 15:28, NKJV; italics added). Celebrating the return of a prodigal is offensive to the ears of an elder brother. Again, just because he shared his father's home did not mean he shared his father's heart.

Once again, the father revealed how he felt and what he thought about his sons. When he saw his youngest son returning home, he ran to him. No lecture was given; no probation period was levied. He was embraced, loved on, and welcomed home. Then we see the father going out to his eldest son, who refused to come in. The father pleaded with his son to come inside and join the cerebration. The love he had for his eldest son was just as strong as his love for his youngest son. The father wanted both of his sons to know that his heart was toward them no matter how they acted at times, when they were lovable and when they were not loveable.

The Elder Son Defends His Position

The eldest son's response to his father's request to join the party reveals that he had the same mindset as his younger brother. He thought like a slave instead of a son. Let me paraphrase what he said to his father. "All these years, I've been *slaving* for you, and you never killed a fatted calf for me so I could have a party with my friends." You cannot live like a son if you think like a slave; plus, I wonder if this young man had any friends to celebrate with. In his moment of anger, he said something that he surely did not believe: "I've never once refused to do a single thing you've told me to do." Really? It is possible to do the right thing with the wrong attitude, and then deceive yourself into thinking all is well.

The elder son did stay home; give him credit for that. But his heart had left his father's house a long time ago. He was there, but he was not there. The motivation for doing what was right did not come from the love he had for his father; it came from the disdain he had for his brother. The contempt for his brother was so deep that he refused to even acknowledge that the father's youngest son was his brother. "But as soon as *this son of yours* came home, who has devoured your livelihood with harlots, you killed the fatted calf for him" (Luke 15:30, NKJV; emphasis added). This son of yours! I wonder who hated to see the prodigal sons return the most, the fatted calf or the elder brother.

The Elder Brother Syndrome

The sandals of the elder brother will fit any one of us; one size fits all. An elder brother is a family member, but he or she does not like to see his or her prodigal brothers and sisters be the recipients of the Father's grace, getting what they do not deserve. Justice, yes, but not grace. An elder brother will be a hard worker and will let you know how hard he or she works. Work, for this person, is not something he or she gets to do; it is something the person has to do. An elder brother will work hard trying to get what he or she already has.

An elder brother has a standard of conduct he or she is committed to, and this person expects others to live up to that standard. If you do not, you may not even be considered a sibling. Elder brothers see themselves as religious experts, pointing out the shortcomings in others when they do not see their own. Anyone who tries to earn his or her right standing before the Father by good works will resent those who receive their right standing before the Father without working for it. It is not fair. I do not know about you; I do not want fairness—give me favor.

The elder son refused to acknowledge any relationship whatsoever with his younger brother. "As soon as *this son of yours* came, who devoured your livelihood with harlots, you killed the fatted calf for him" (Luke 15:30, NKJV; emphasis added). He may be your son, but he is not my brother. An elder bother will adjudicate in the court of his or her own opinion who is and who is not a part of the family. Family membership will not be determined by birth; that decision will be made by the elder brother. Facts will not encumber his or her decisions, either.

The classic trait of an elder brother is exposure: "Yet when this son of yours comes back from squandering your money on prostitutes, you celebrate by killing the fattened calf" (Luke 15:30, NLT). These words never came out of the father's mouth because they were not in the father's heart. *"For out of the abundance of the heart the mouth speaks"* (Matthew 12:34, NKJV; italics added). The elder brother exposed what the father covered, and in doing so, he revealed his heart. A believer who is manifesting the elder brother syndrome will not only expose the sins of a brother or sister; he or she will get some twisted satisfaction in doing so. An elder brother will not mind airing out another sibling's dirty laundry.

Love covers, and that is exactly what the father did when his youngest son came home dirty, soiled, and stained from his involvement with the world: he covered him with the best robe. This pathetic reprobate found acceptance and forgiveness from the father.

This is precisely why the elder brother was so ticked off. How dare they celebrate a sinner's return? An elder brother and a judgmental spirit are inseparable. This boy's affection was not for his father; it was for the material things his father had. Love for his father was not what kept him home; it was his love for his father's stuff.

The Father's Heart for His Elder Son

We spend a lot of time talking about the two boys in this parable, when the spotlight should actually be on the father. His love for both of his sons never wavered. The elder son was given the same things his younger brother received, and he did not even realize it. He was given grace. The father extended grace to both of them. They were sons by birth, and that is the only way the father could treat them.

The father reminds his eldest son who he is and what he has. *"Son, you're always with me and all that I have is yours"* (Luke 15:31, NKJV; italics added). Instead of calling him a knucklehead, he affectionately called him a son. In doing so, the father reminded him of his birthright. He was a son by birth, and that entitled him to everything the father had. He got to share his father's home, and he got to share his father's heart. As a matter of fact, when the youngest son demanded his portion of the father's livelihood, we are told, "So *he divided to them* his livelihood" (Luke 15:12, NKJV; emphasis added). When the youngest son got his portion, the elder son got his portion too. An elder brother usually has a short memory. It is hard to enjoy what you have when you are focused on what others are doing with what they have.

The father told his eldest son that cerebrating the homecoming of his brother was the right thing to do. Children of the father belong in the father's house and in the father's presence. The father lovingly reminded the elder brother of his family ties: "For *your brother* was dead and is alive again, and was lost and is found" (Luke 15:32, NKJV; emphasis added). This is your brother we are talking about. This is not a time to be fussing and fighting; it is a time to be partying.

Does Jesus Leave Us Hanging?

The story ends a little weird. We would like to think the elder son finally came to his senses and joined the celebration. Surely the two sons reconciled their differences with one another, fell in love with their father, and lived happily ever after. That is not how Jesus ended the story. He leaves us in suspense, or did He?

Place yourself in the story as a listener. Pretend you are a part of the crowd that day, listening to Jesus talk about the lost sheep, the lost piece of silver, and the two sons. Whose sandals are you wearing, the son who left the father and lived a life of sin, or the son who stayed home and continued to work hard? Who are you relating to, the son who did the wrong things, or the son who did the right thing?

This crowd of listeners were offended and very upset with Jesus for suggesting that the Father would accept sinners unconditionally and love them so extravagantly. That flew in the face of their religion. After all, they each had worked hard for their positions of right standing. Their love was not for the Father but for what they got out of the relationship with the Father. They knew all about the Father, but they did not know the Father. Work was more important to them than worship. Work is about who we are; worship is about who He is.

This same spirit is prevalent within the body of Christ today. There is no shortage of elder brothers, working so hard to get what they have already been given. Hard work is to be commended, but it should never be a substitute for worship. We work because we get to work, not because we have to work. We are sons, not slaves. The work that we do comes out of our beings; we are not working to become who we already are. This is precisely why so many believers become tired and worn out. When this happens, we are left with two options. We either quit, or we begin to pretend. An elder brother will keep doing what he or she is doing long after his or her heart has left home. Going through the motions will give the appearance of being a faithful child, but the person is really a slave. It is hard to live like a son when you think like a slave.

If we only knew that it is possible to share our Father's home but not share our Father's heart.

If We Only Knew

Count It All Joy
When Your Faith Is Tested

BEING A CHILD OF GOD DOES NOT CHANGE WHAT WE HAVE TO DEAL with in life. What does change is how we deal with it. As long as we are in this world, we will go through some difficult times. It is not *if* trouble comes; it is *when* trouble comes. Life can be unfair. Good things can happen to bad people, and bad things can happen to good people. It is possible to do all the right things, push the right buttons, pull the right levers, and still have life fall in on you. The Lord did not promise the world would treat us fairly. He did promise He would never leave or forsake us. In this life, we will have troubles, but we are told to rejoice because He has overcome the world. Life does not have to be fair.

Why do bad things happen to good people? If God is fair, then why does He allow good people to suffer? This question is asked all the time by people who do not know God or by those who are still very immature in their faith. It is still a legitimate question that begs to be answered. It is not actually a question about the fairness of God; it is about the fallen condition of the world in which we live. Jesus said that sunlight is given to the bad and to the good. It rains on the just and the unjust (Matthew 5:45, NKJV). The bad receive the benefits of the sunlight and rain, as do the good. What happens to people, both good and bad, is based on them being in this world, not because they are good or bad or that God is fair or unfair. It is about living in a world that has been soiled and corrupted by sin.

Adam's disobedience affected the entire human race. Not only did Adam fall when he disobeyed God by eating fruit from the forbidden tree; he took the entire human race down with him. His sin contaminated all of creation as well. Every person who has been born from the time of Adam has been born estranged from God. The fruit from his rebellion against God is a sinful world filled with sinful people. The reason bad things sometimes happen to good people is not because God is unfair; it is because Adam did what God told him not to do.

If you see a sign that says "Do not touch, wet paint," and you disobey the sign's command and get paint all over yourself, whose fault is it? Do you blame the one who put the sign up or the one who refused to follow the warning? The sign was posted out of the goodness of a person's heart to prevent people from getting paint on themselves. The one who refused to adhere to the sign's warning is the one at fault.

Out of the goodness of His nature, God told Adam not to eat from the tree of the knowledge of good and evil because He knew what would happen if Adam disobeyed. It was not the goodness of God that caused the problem; it was the badness of humanity.

This was the purpose for Jesus coming to the earth, to give fallen humanity the opportunity to step back into in obedience, what Adam stepped out of in disobedience. Once a person accepts Christ and receives Him as his or her personal Lord and Savior, the person is a new creation, but he or she is still living in the same old corrupt world. This is what Jesus meant when He said that we are in the world, but we are not of the world. Being in the world means we are subjected to troubles and difficulties even though we are now children of God.

Bad things can and do happen to good people, but it is not because God is unfair; it is because good people live in a sinful world. Being a new creation in Christ does not change *what* we have to deal with in life, but *how* we deal with it.

Troubles Are Inevitable, and They Have a Purpose

It is impossible to go through life unscathed. In writing to the Jews who had been driven from their homes and from their homeland because of their faith in Christ, James said, "My brethren, count it all joy *when* you fall into various trials" (James 1:2, NKJV; emphasis added). Notice that James did not say *if* you have trials. He said *when* you have trials. Trials are like death and taxes. It is not if you die or if you pay taxes, it is when. Trials are inevitable.

James uses the word *various* in describing trials. We get our English word *polka dot* from this word. That is an interesting choice of words. Trials are like polka dots: they come in all colors and sizes. Life has its testing times, and when they come, James says that we can face them with a mindset of joy. That is possible only if we know who we are in Christ and what is going on when difficult times hit.

"*Knowing* that *the testing of your faith* produces patience" (James 1:3, NKJV; emphasis added). You are never the object of a test; your faith is. The troubles we find ourselves going through are for the purpose of strengthening our faith, not destroying us.

To understand what James is saying about the testing of your faith, think about your child taking swimming lessons. At the end of the lessons, the swimming instructor will give your child a test to validate his or her ability to swim. As a proud parent, you are there to cheer him or her on. While your child is swimming along the edge of the pool, the instructor is walking alongside clapping his or her hands and shouting words of encouragement to your child: "You can make it! Good job. Keep kicking. You're doing well. You're almost there." The swimming test is to approve the child, not to destroy him or her.

I have never heard about a swimming instructor who walked beside a swimmer being tested, saying things like, "Drown, you little rat. You're not going to make it. Give up." The instructor is for your child and the test is to approve them, not to destroy them.

This is what James is saying about the testing of our faith. When our faith is tested, it is for the purpose of validation. Our endurance has a chance to grow and mature when we find ourselves going through difficult moments. During these testing times, Holy Spirit is rooting us on. "You can make it. You're doing well. Keep believing. Don't give up."

Tough Times Don't Last; Tough People Do

When I was growing up, I remember hearing people say when things were going south, "Cheer up. Things could get worse." This was said in an attempt to lighten the moment. Sometimes the response would be, "I cheered up, and sure enough, things got worse." The thing about tough times is that they do not last forever. At times, they may seem like they will never end, especially if you are the one in the fray. Have you noticed that the struggle is not as long for others as it is for you?

I find incredible comfort from the words of Psalms 30. The Psalmist is praising and thanking God for His faithfulness in keeping him on his feet when life was trying to knock him down. Out of the crucible of his trials and tribulation come these words: *"Weeping may endure for a night, but joy comes in the morning"* (Psalms 30:5, NKJV; italics added). The joy of the morning will chase away the weeping that was done in the night. Our heavenly Father turns our mourning into dancing. Tough times do not last; tough people do.

Life Is Full of Curve Balls

The count was three and two. What happened next was not expected by the coaches, the fans, and especially the batter. The pitch was a wicked slow curve that caught the batter totally off guard for strike three. I will never forget what the announcer said in describing that moment: "That wasn't fair." A curve ball is very effective when you are not expecting it. As a matter of fact, if you are convinced the next pitch will be a fastball, you can easily get suckered by a curveball. That's life. Life can set you up. Sometimes life just ain't fair.

Life is kind of like marriage. You did not find what you were expecting, and you did not expect what you found. You thought it would be moonlight and roses, but it turned out to be daylight and dishes. Sometimes there are more bills than thrills. This is reality.

I heard a pastor say once, "When you find yourself in a time of tribulation, there's only one thing to do: tribulate" (Lobius Murray). Well, that sounds simple enough, but I am not sure what that means. I have a few thoughts, but I will keep them to myself for the time being.

If we are not careful, we can become critical of those who may be dealing with an unfair circumstance. I am sure you have heard folks say things like, "If that were me ..." or "I would never ..." or "You would never catch me ..." The truth is, we really do not know what we would do in any situation until we find ourselves in it.

Several years ago, Jori Buchenau, a dear pastor friend of mine, posted something on Facebook about his ten-year old-son that melted my heart. "Coy was born three months premature (23 weeks) and weighed only 1 lb. 8 oz. He has cerebral palsy and is legally blind." What his dad wrote about his son moved me deeply. I asked for and received his permission to share this story. As a matter of fact, here are his own words sent to me in a text. "Permission joyfully granted. We want to use the same arrows the enemy shoots at us as our ammunition to annihilate his kingdom. He (the enemy) cannot have our zoe (life). Coy had a seizure at 6:00 am [*sic*] this morning, first one in six months. After he woke up, he said, 'Can I praise the Lord now?' That's my boy! No weapon formed against him shall prosper."

Can I praise the Lord now! It is not fair for innocent children to suffer, but many do. My friend's son's response should be our response when life is not treating us fairly. We should praise the Lord in the midst of the unfairness. Our response to life's unfair treatment should be, "We will praise the Lord now!"

Here is something we need to get a handle on. It is possible to do the right thing, do it with a good attitude, and still have things fall apart. You can live right, think right, and do right, and things can blow up in your face. I know some bad people who seemly have it good, and I know some good people who are going through some tough times. This is not fair. But nowhere in the bible does it say life is fair or has to be fair. As long as we are in this world, we will have trials and testing times. It is not because our God is unfair or is not good. It is because of humanity's disobedience to God's warning not to eat from the forbidden tree. God posted the sign, but humans ignored the warning and touched the wet paint. All the unfairness and evil in the world that affects every person, both the good and the bad, is humanity's fault—not Gods.

Life is filled with moments when we feel the squeeze of a test. When this happens, we need to remember what James told us. We are not the object of the test; our faith is. Various trials are cleansing moments designed to flush out the toxins that have secretly invaded our lives. There will be those moments when we get to see if we are just talk, or if we really believe what we say we believe.

If we only knew that we can face life's testing times with a mindset of joy, knowing that we are not the object of the test—our faith is.

If We Only Knew

All We Need Is an Ear to Hear and a Leg to Stand On

QUITTING IS AN OPTION, BUT NOT FOR A WINNER. IT WAS VINCE Lombardi who said, "Winners never quit, and quitters never win." How true that is. Sometimes, life has a way of knocking the spiritual wind out of our sails, leaving us stunned and emotionally adrift. When that happens, throwing in the towel can become an attractive option.

There is an interesting and colorful verse in the book of Amos where the prophet is describing Israel's predicament. They were on the verge of annihilation. Their enemies had them surrounded and were determined to wipe them off the face of the earth. God said they would suffer great loss, but He would come to their rescue and deliver them, even if there was only a smidgen of them left. "As a shepherd takes from the mouth of a lion *two legs or a piece of an ear*, so shall the children of Israel be taken out Who dwell in Samaria. In the corner of a bed and on the edge of a couch" (Amos 3:12, NKJV; emphasis added).

A lion may attack the flock and kill one of the sheep, but a good shepherd will fight to retrieve what is left of the sheep, even if it is only a couple of legs and a piece of an ear. Here is what we need to glean from what the prophet Amos said. Even though life events can leave us devastated at times, as long as we have an ear to hear and a leg to stand on, it's not over! We can keep living even when everything in us wants to quit. "Our greatest weakness lies in giving up. The most certain way to succeed is always to try just one more time" (Thomas Edison).

The Scent of Hope

Oftentimes in the scriptures, a tree or trees are used as a metaphor for people. Keep this in mind as you read the following passage. "For there is *hope for a tree* [person], if it is cut down, that it will sprout again, and that its tender shoots [life] will not cease. Though its root may grow old in the earth [it may take some time], and its stump may die in the ground, yet *at the scent of water* it will bud and bring forth branches like a plant" (Job 14:7–9, NKJV; emphasis added).

All it takes for a dormant life to spring up again is a scent, the scent of hope. You cannot see a scent. You sense a scent. Living in the Panhandle of Texas, we know something about drought. Sometimes we have prolonged periods of time when we receive little to no rain. During some of these dry spells, the hope that farmers have for a good crop begins to wane. All it takes for their hopes to rise again is to catch a whiff of moisture, the scent of rain. You cannot see it, but you can sure smell it. Something on the outside stimulates something on the inside. The scent of rain causes hope to rise.

The writer of Proverbs says, "Hope deferred makes the heart sick, but when the desire comes, it is a tree of life" (Proverbs 13:12, NKJV). Hope is confident expectation of what God has promised. The strength of hope is in His faithfulness to His promises. Hope and faith is what motivates us to keep going when everything within us is screaming for us to quit. When a person has hope, they have faith. To have hope is believing things will get better (hope), even though we cannot prove it will get better (faith). If a person's hope can be put on hold, their faith can be stolen. It is possible to have faith without hope, but it is impossible to have hope without faith.

This is why the writer of Proverbs says, "Hope deferred makes the heart [soul] sick" (Proverbs 13:12, NKJV; emphasis added). To defer something is to place it on hold, to postpone. It is like having your vacation plans tossed up in the air because of some unforeseen event that is out of your control. "But when the desire comes, it is a tree of life" (Proverbs 13:12, NKJV). The scent of hope turns life around. "Faith is the confidence that what we hope for will actually happen; it gives us assurance about things we cannot see" (Hebrews 11:1, NLT).

Our Way Out of Hopelessness

The community of faith is filled with people who have untapped potential, but because of unrelenting disappointments, their hope has been placed on hold. When hope is deferred, potential remains just that, potential. A person can take all his or her hope and unfulfilled dreams to the grave. Without hope, a person is like a ship without power, left to the mercies of the wind. Too many of our brothers and sisters in Christ are drifting around aimlessly, believing the lie that life is not worth living. It makes it so much easier for a person to throw in the towel when he or she has no confident expectation that life will get better. Decisions that are made when hope is ebbing can have devastating consequences.

We have a proclivity to judge what will happen tomorrow based on what happens today. If our hope is determined by the good or the bad that we experience during any given day, we will be jerked around like a kite on a string in high wind, sailing along nicely one moment and then nose-diving the next. This is why the word of God tells us to place our focus on Jesus, because He is the author and finisher of our faith.

Hope, or the lack of it, is determined by what we choose to focus our attention on. It is a choice. We can look at how big our problems are, or we can focus on how big our God is. Someone once said, don't tell God how big your problem is; tell your problem how big your God is. That may be a simple way to say it, but it is packed with truth.

There is only one way out of hopelessness, and that way is Jesus. Jesus said that He is the door, the gate, and the way. A door makes it possible for us to enter or egress something. Jesus is our way of escaping hopelessness, and He is our entrance in to hope. Jesus is the only one who has the power to take "lessness" out of hope. As our door, He makes it possible for us to escape the enemy of despair and enter His joy. "The joy of the Lord is our strength" (Nehemiah 8:10, NKJV). This is why the writer of Hebrews tells us to keep our eyes on Jesus: He is the one who initiates and perfects our faith.

There is another reason we are instructed to keep our focus on Jesus. He is our example. He did not quit! If anyone had a legitimate reason to give up, to throw in the towel, it was Him. Instead, He endured the cross and ignored the shame, so we would have a way of escape from every weapon the enemy forms and uses against us. The beating He took for you and for me cannot be described adequately. One translation says that He was beaten so severely, He could not be recognized as being human (Isaiah 52:14, NLT). He was disfigured beyond recognition. Jesus endured so that no matter what we may find ourselves going through, as long as we have an ear to hear and a leg to stand on, it is not over!

All a person needs for life to turn around is to have a sudden good break. Jesus was broken for us so we could have that break. Keep your eyes fastened on Him. "Unrelenting disappointment can leave a person's heart sick but a sudden good break can turn life around" (Proverbs, 13:12; NLT).

Lessons Learned in the Dark

I have found that some of my greatest spiritual growth seasons have taken place in my nighttime experiences. I am sure you have noticed that you can see the stars only when it is dark. How much beauty of God's incredible creation would we miss if we never saw the dark? Sometimes it takes a sunset to enjoy the sunrise.

Eleanor Roosevelt, along with several others, said, "It is better to light a candle than to curse the darkness." A candle may appear to be a small answer to a big problem, but it is the first step in the right direction. The candle in a dark moment of our lives is the giving of thanks. It may seem small in comparison to the problems we are facing, but it is the first step in the right direction from hopelessness to hope. The Lord never tells us to thank Him *for all things*; He tells us to *thank Him in all things*. You may find yourself in a dark moment right now, but go ahead and light a small candle of thanksgiving and see what it eventually does to the darkness that is closing in on you. It is the choice of giving thanks that keeps things in perspective for us, especially when life has thrown us a curveball.

In the very beginning of the beginning, there was darkness before there was light, nighttime was before daytime (Genesis 1:1–5, NKJV). Pay attention to the significance of order. The day chases the night away. Light dispels the darkness. If day had been first, then darkness would chase away light. "Weeping may last through the night but joy comes in the morning" (Psalms 30:5, NKJV).

Sometimes, the best ideas and thoughts I have happen in the nighttime experiences of my life. This is why we must not allow our feelings and thoughts to become our realities. Our valley-of-the-shadow-of-death experiences have a way of tainting truth. We have the tendency to focus on the valley of death, and we cannot see the presence of the shadow. Without light, there cannot be a shadow. That tells me where Jesus is during my dark moments. He is walking with me through the valley of the shadow of death; this is why I will not fear. Feelings and emotions are real, but they may not be true. Reality is what God says. He said that He would never leave or forsake us (Hebrews 13:5, NKJV).

Some of the best teaching moments occur when life seems to be at its darkest. Don't curse the darkness; praise the light. Let hope rise.

Lies of the Darkness

Once you start believing the lies of darkness: "You will never be happy," "Life will never turn around for you," "You're a loser," "No one really loves or cares about you," "You'll never see the light again," we lose our ears to hear. These words, and words like these, are never from your loving heavenly Father. They come from the lying lips of the enemy, and he uses a familiar voice to give them the sound of legitimacy.

I cannot tell you how many believers I have ministered to over the last fifty years who have left the fellowship of the community of faith because they got their feelings hurt. I hear them say things like, "No one appreciated me," "All they were after was my money," "I wasn't getting fed,", "So-and-so talked about me behind my back," "The pastor snubbed me," "No one ever included me in their clique," ad infinitum. When people say things like this, it tells me where their focus has been, and it has not been on the shadow (Lord). Most are not happy with my response, but what I say to them is said in love. Do you think anyone has ever left the church because of you? Have you ever talked about anyone behind his or her back? The only person I know that has to be fed is a baby. What are you saying about yourself when you say you are not being fed?

When we take our focus off Jesus and place it on people, things, churches, and ministries, we are setting ourselves up to become victims of the enemy's scams. We have no one to blame but ourselves. We do not have a leg to stand on or an ear to hear.

Our Way Out of Darkness

It is easy to get trapped in hopelessness, but it is easy to take the "lessness" out of hope. We praise our way out. Praise is the light that chases the darkness away. When the candle of praise is lit, darkness cannot stay, no matter how faint the light may be at first. Praise is not a feeling. If it were, we probably would not do much of it because when you are in a dark moment, you do not feel like offering up a sacrifice of praise; but that is precisely what praise is when we do not feel like it—it is a sacrifice.

The enemy is the one who has inserted the "lessness" in hope, and he knows you will shake it off if you choose to worship and praise your heavenly Father, especially when you do not feel like it. This is why he will whisper in your ear that you are being hypercritical when you are worshiping God when you do not feel like it. The truth is, the moments when you choose not to worship God because you do not feel like it are when you are being hypocritical. Being a hypocrite is pretending to be something you are not. Worshipping is who you are!

One of my all-time favorite baseball players was George Herman "Babe" Ruth Jr. He died five months before I was born. One of my most treasured baseball cards was the one I had of "the Babe." Here is one of his many quotable quotes: "You just can't beat the person who won't give up." The enemy cannot beat the child of God who will not give up. Worship and praise the Lord when you feel like it, but more importantly, worship and praise Him when you do not feel like it. Praise and worship will be the way out of your dark moment.

Being honest with ourselves just may be the most difficult thing we can do. Knowing our shortcomings is not the issue; acknowledging them is. If you find yourself in a spiritual fog right now, if your vision of your present and future is clouded, you may be in the best position you could possibly find yourself in for an exponential faith growth spurt. I read something years ago that has stuck with me. When there is nothing left but you and Jesus, you have just enough to start over. Quitting is an option, but not for a winner. You are a winner.

Difficult times can actually be a blessing in disguise because we get to see God right in the middle of our difficulties. Most of us were drawn to the Lord through the difficulties we were going through. My personal relationship with the Lord has deepened because of the challenges and struggles He has walked me through. It is weird but true; tough times can actually be our greatest blessings.

If we only knew that we already have what it takes to live a victorious life and that not only can we survive our death-valley seasons, we can actually thrive in spite of them. All it takes to live in hope is a leg to stand on and an ear to hear: He who has an ear, let him hear.

If We Only Knew
Christ Is Our Life

"You do what you can as long as you can, and when you can't, you do the next best thing. You back up but you don't give up" (Chuck Yeager). This may be one of my all-time favorite quotes. Chuck Yeager was a United States Air Force officer and a flying ace. In 1947, he became the first pilot in history to exceed the speed of sound in level flight. What was so remarkable about General Yeager is that he began his career in the United States Air Force as a private in World War II. Chuck Yeager is truly a great American.

There is no telling how many times I have used General Yeager's quote to inspire the kids I coached in baseball, basketball, and football. The crux of the quote is, "You never give up." There may be times when you may have to step back and take an assessment of the situation, but quitting is not an option, because as Yogi Berra said, "It's not over till it's over."

A never-say-die attitude is an admirable quality, and possessing this kind of spunk will get you through a lot of tough spots. But as a child of God, it will take you to the brink of burnout and despair. I have heard the following statement said by Christians far more times than I want to recall: "Living the Christian life is so hard. I don't think I can keep it up." I have news for you: living the Christian life is not hard; it is impossible to live. God designed it that way.

"Do what you can as long as you can, and when you can't, you'll start pretending or you'll quit" (Wayne Kniffen). Church buildings are filled with believers who have given up on living the victorious Christian life. They are still attending services, singing with the praise team, giving money, working, and preaching, but they are just going through the motions. Their bodies may still be in the building but their hearts left a long time ago. They have surrendered. The white flag has been hoisted to the top of the pole. When you do the best you can, for as long as you can, the day will come when you can't.

Dead Man Living

"For in Him (Jesus) we live and move and have our being, as also some of your own poets have said, "For we are also His offspring'" (Acts 17:28, NKJV; emphasis added). This verse can be summed up in four words, *Christ is our life*. Christ lives His life through dead people.

If it were possible to live the life that was required by the Old Covenant, you would have to be God. The requirement of the law is nothing short of perfection. If it were possible to live the life of the New Covenant of grace, you would not need God. Both the Old Covenant (law) and the New Covenant (grace) are not only difficult to live; they are impossible to live. This is by God's design. The new life we have in Christ is designed to be lived by dead people.

In his letter to the church at Galatia, Paul says, "I am crucified with Christ; and it is no longer I who live, but it is Christ who lives in me" (Galatians 2:20, NKJV). If the truth of this verse ever takes root in the inner cores of our beings, we will not only survive whatever life throws at us, but we will thrive no matter what season we may find ourselves in. Pay attention to what Paul says. He does not say he is trying to live in a Christ-like way or that he is living a life that brings glory to Christ. What he does say is that Christ is living His life through him. The Christian life is not about behaving like Christ; it is believing that Christ is living His life through us. The Christian life is not about us living like dead people; it is about Jesus living His life through dead people. When this becomes our reality, we will live in a way that brings glory to Christ, because our focus will be on who Christ has made us to be and not on doing to become like Christ.

In no way am I making light of the importance of living a godly life. But if the godly life we are trying to live is by our behavior, then we will do all we can, the best we can, for as long as we can, and when we can't do it any longer, we will quit.

When we accepted Christ and received Him as our Lord and Savior, He came to live in the deepest parts of our inner-most beings, our spirits. We now have a new life in Christ, and He is the source of our new lives. In our souls, we can choose to ignore Him as the source of our new lives. Our souls are our minds, emotions, and will. What we think, how we feel, and what we do comes out of our souls. In our souls, we can choose to ignore Him as the source of our new life and continue to live much like we did before we were born from above. Christ is in us, but He can be limited by us because He has given us a free will.

Christ not only lives in us; He wants to express Himself through us. He does this through our souls, our thinking, through our feelings and our will, and what we do. This is why Jesus said, *"If you've seen Me you've seen the Father"* (John 14:9, NKJV; italics added). The Father lived His life through Jesus as Jesus.

"Then *Christ will make His home in your hearts* as you trust Him. Your roots will grow down into God's love and keep you strong" (Ephesians 3:17, NLT; emphasis added). Our heart is Christ's home, and He wants full run of the house. When we realize we are dead and that Christ is living His life through us as us, we will be strong no matter what life throws at us. The victorious Christian life is not about doing what you can, the best you can, for as long as you can; it is realizing that you can't, but that He can!

Christ Is Our Way—Christ Is Our Truth—Christ Is Our Life

"Since you have been raised to new life with Christ, set your sights on the realities of heaven, where Christ sits in the place of honor at God's right hand. Think about the things of heaven, not the things of earth. *For you died to this life, and your real life is hidden with Christ in God.* And when *Christ, Who is your life,* is revealed to the whole world, you will share in all His glory" (Colossians 3:1–4, NLT; emphasis added). This passage of scripture is a treasure trove of biblical information concerning our identities as believers. Paul is very clear and concise in what he says in these four verses about the new lives we have been given: Christ is our life. He does not accept us just to become a part of our lives. He is not a spiritual trophy that we add to our trophy case. Without Him, we have no lives. This is precisely why the bible says that a person who is not a believer is already dead. "For the message of the cross is foolishness to those *who are perishing,* but to us who are being saved it is the power of God" (1 Corinthians 1:18, NKJV; emphasis added). Paul does not say that the message of the cross *appears to be foolishness* to those who will perish someday; he says the message of the cross *is foolishness* to those who are perishing now. The unsaved are already dead, waiting for the second death.

It is possible to know a lot about Christ and not really to know Him. We should never confuse information with transformation. Information without transformation is just that, information. Just because an individual can quote a lot of scripture does not mean he or she knows the God of the scriptures. Jesus said in John 14:6 (NKJV) that He was the way, the truth, and the life. Without Him, there is no going. Without Him, there is no knowing. Without Him, there is no growing. Christ is our way; Christ is our truth; Christ is our life.

When we had our born-from-above experience with Christ, we did not just receive a new life; we received Christ, who is our life. This may give the appearance of splitting hairs, but maybe the hairs need to be split. Our tendency is to separate the things of God from God.

Wayne Kniffen

When we accepted Christ as our way, we accepted Him because He is our way; not something distinct from Him. When we accepted Him as our life, we got Him because He is life.

The streets were crowded; people were jostling one another as Jesus and His disciples were making their way to the home of Jairus, whose twelve-year-old daughter was at the brink of death. Out of the crowd, a hand slowly reached out and touched the border of Jesus's clothes. It was the hand of a woman who had a medical issue that could not be resolved by physicians. She had been fighting this battle for twelve years and had spent everything she had. Being in public with this particular health issue was in violation of the law. She was desperate. When desperation sets in, most restraints are easily cast aside. I am sure she felt like Jesus was her last hope. The truth is, Jesus was her only hope.

The instant her hand touched Jesus, she was immediately healed. I cannot imagine what she must have felt at that moment. I also cannot imagine what her thoughts were when Jesus said, "Who touched Me?" (Luke 8:45, NKJV), She was caught. Peter, the spokesman for the band of disciples, responded with, "Lord, everybody is touching you. This is a huge crowd, everybody is bumping into everybody, and You say, who touched Me" (Luke 8:45, NKJV; paraphrased).

What Jesus said next was tantamount to understanding that Christ is our life. *"Someone touched Me, for I perceived power going out from Me"* (Luke 8:46, NKJV; italics added). The New Living Translation says, *"Someone deliberately touched Me for I felt healing power go out from Me"* (Luke 8:46, NLT; italics added). It was not this woman's physical touch that got Jesus's attention; her faith touched Him. It was her faith that caused Jesus to say, "Who touched me?"

Our inclination is to see the healing that came out of Jesus as something separate from Jesus. For us to see it that way is to see healing as a thing and not a person. Jesus is not only our healer; more importantly, He is our healing. He is our life. The power that Jesus felt leave Him was not something that was separate from Him; it was Him. Jesus was her healing.

128

After the woman saw that she could not hide, she came trembling and fell down at the feet of Jesus. In front of all the people, she told Him the reason she had touched Him and how she was immediately healed. This lady took a risk in believing that Jesus was her way, Jesus was her truth, and that Jesus was her life. Jesus was her healing.

Our Union with Christ

I love some of the new worship songs that are being written today. The Lord has blessed us with some incredibly gifted young Christian song writers, who are more interested in the heart of worship than they are with the art of worship. This is so important for the health of the body of Christ, to have songs that are focused on Jesus and Jesus alone. Every time I hear two of these songs in particular, my entire being senses His presence in me, and all I want to do is sit at His feet and tell Him how much I love Him. I become keenly aware that Christ is my life and that His love for me is unshakable. Once you realize He is your life, everything else fades away. When you lock into His presence, you never want to leave. He becomes more important to you than things are. Priorities are rearranged and desires are realigned when we become aware that He is all we want and that He is all we need. In His presence, we become aware that what we have in Christ is more than a relationship; we are in union with Him.

In Genesis 2, we find a verse that is not only interesting, but it seems to be out of place. "Therefore, a man shall leave his father and mother and be joined to his wife, and *they shall become one flesh*" (Genesis 2:24, NKJV; emphasis added). In the very beginning of time, God gives humankind instructions about leaving their fathers and mothers before there were fathers and mothers. There is a special dynamic between a man and his wife. They are in union with one another. This is why we use the term marriage union, because it is more than a relationship.

We may not grasp what God means by union, but I assure you, the enemy of your soul does. When the devil was negotiating for the right to come against Job, in order to prove he was faithful to God only because of how God had blessed him, God gave Satan permission with restrictions. Satan was given access to Job and everything he owned, but he was forbidden from taking his life.

The enemy's attack on Job was savage. He lost everything, including his health. On second thought, he did not lose everything. He did not lose his wife. Have you ever wondered why? The enemy who is out to defeat and destroy God's people knows what most Christians do not know. He understands union. When he heard God say that he could not kill Job, he understood that he could not kill Job's wife either. Why? They were one; they were in union with one another.

Union is the heart and soul of the doctrine of salvation. When you accepted Jesus and received Him as your Lord and Savior, you were included in the greatest mystery that has ever transpired—the Incarnation. Being in union with Christ is the central truth of the new-creation life. "We have become partakers of His divine nature" (2 Peter 1:4, NKJV). Christ is our life.

What is the incarnation? Simply stated, it is deity wrapped up in humanity. Jesus was God wrapped up in human flesh. Christ was His divinity, and Jesus was His humanity. In theology, this is called the hypostatic union, divinity, and humanity in one.

Being a partaker of His divine nature looks like this: Christ is in you; you are in Christ. Divinity is living in humanity. "In Him [Christ] we live and move and have our being" (Acts 17:28, NKJV; emphasis added). Christ not only has given us a new life; He is our life. If that will not make you shout, your shouter is broke.

If we only knew who we are in Christ, our lives would be different. "As *He is, so are we* in this world" (1 John 4:17, NKJV; emphasis added).

18

If We Only Knew
Ignorance May Not Be Bliss

"Ignorance is bliss" is a proverb that means, if you do not know something, it is of no concern to you. I have heard it said this way: what you don't know won't hurt you (Margaret Atwood). That may be true in some cases, but when it comes to knowing who we are as children of God, what we do not know can and does hurt us. The enemy of our souls is wreaking havoc on the body of Christ today because of our ignorance concerning our identities as believers. The prophet Hosea may be considered a minor prophet, but he wrote something major when he penned these words, "My people are destroyed for a lack of knowledge" (Hosea 4:6, NKJV). Destruction comes because of a lack of knowledge. What was true in the middle of the eighth century BC is still true in the twenty-first century. God's people are being scammed, and we don't even know it.

In writing to the church in Ephesus, Paul says, "Therefore I, a prisoner for serving the Lord, beg you to lead a life worthy of your calling, for you have been called by God" (Ephesians 4:1, NLT). Even in the early stages of Christianity, the people of God were not living up to their identities as believers. It is hard to live up to what you do not know. The devil knows he cannot undo what God has done in your life, but he also knows that if he can keep you in the dark as to what God has done in your life, you will never live up to your identity as a new creation. If the enemy is successful in keeping us in the dark as to who we are in Christ, we will remain in ignorance, and we will not live up to our calling. We may have some short seasons of successful living, but for the most part, we will live in defeat. The devil is a scam artist and an identity thief.

Here is some good news. There is an awakening within the body of Christ about what happened to a person when he or she had his or her born-from-above experience. The Holy Spirit is bringing an incredible revelation about identity to those who are hungry to know. God does fill the heart of the hungry with good things (Luke 1:53, NKJV). We need to pay attention. It is a matter of remaining ignorant or choosing to be … You fill in the blank.

Ignorance Exposed

Ignorance is not knowing something. Remaining ignorant is not wanting to know something. It is one thing not to know who you are as a child of God; it is another thing to not want to know who you are as a child of God. I realize this may be an over simplification of the term *ignorant*, but my purpose is to make a point. I love what Benjamin Franklin said, "We are all born ignorant but one must work hard to remain ignorant." I am not using the word *ignorant* as an adjective to describe a person or people in general. This word is used to elucidate the extremes of not knowing something and not wanting to know. That something is our new identities as children of God.

When we were born again, our understanding of what happened to us was limited. We certainly knew something was not the same, but as far as our new identities goes, we were still ignorant. When a baby is born, what does it know about what happened to it? I think the answer is obvious—not a thing. The baby has to be taught how he or she came into this world as he or she grows and matures as a human being. A person who has had a born-from-above experience, has to be taught what happened to him or her and who Christ has made the person to be. It is impossible to rule and reign in this life if we remain ignorant or if we choose not to know our new birth identities.

In his teaching on what happens to a child of God when the person dies, Paul writes, "But I do not want you to be ignorant brethren, concerning those who have fallen asleep, lest you sorrow as others who have no hope" (1 Thessalonians 4:13, NKJV). Paul was not talking down to the people when he said that he did not want them to be ignorant. That was certainly not his spirit. Paul did not want the believers in Thessalonica, who were the recipients of this letter, to be without knowledge concerning what happens to a believer when the individual dies. They just did not know, and if you don't know, you don't know.

In his description of Gentile unbelievers to the church at Ephesus, Paul writes, *"Having their_understanding darkened, being alienated from the life of God, because of the ignorance that is in them, because of the blindness of their heart"* (Ephesians 4:18, NKJV; emphasis added). Because these unbelieving Gentiles were ignorant and their hearts were full of darkness, they were given over to an ungodly lifestyle. Ignorance is not always bliss. It can be very costly.

"O foolish Galatians! Who has bewitched you that you should not obey the truth, before whose eyes Jesus Christ was clearly portrayed among you as crucified?" (Galatians 3:1, NKJV; emphasis added). Instead of the word *foolish*, Paul could have used the synonym *dumb*. What is important to keep in mind when you read this is that Paul loved these people. He was not in any way being disrespectful or cruel. The word *foolish* carries with it the idea of knowing the truth, seeing the truth, but still believing a lie. The Christians in Galatia knew the truth about their identities as believers. They knew their new lives began by grace and not by works, but someone had convinced them to abandon that truth and to rely on their good works in order

to keep themselves in right standing with God. They were trying to keep by their good works what they did not get by their good works— right standing with God. This is why Paul called them foolish. He is speaking truth in love.

It is one thing to not know who you are as a child of God; it is another thing to not want to know who you are as a child of God. Ignorance can have a lot of negative consequences, but not wanting to know can be devastating. Both are a choice.

My Personal Story of Denial

It was Sunday morning, Valentine's Day. As I was concluding my message, it felt like my heart inverted in my chest. The pain almost took me to the carpet. I knew something had happened, and I knew it was not good. Quickly dismissing the service, I hastily made my way to my office so I would not have to deal with anyone. I was in excruciating pain!

I had been having symptoms of heart issues for several months. Every time I felt an unusual pain of heaviness in my chest and aching in my elbows and left forearm, I dismissed it as fatigue, even though, deep down inside, I was fairly sure it was my heart. I just did not want to admit it. I knew, but I did not want to know.

My Valentine's Day episode gradually eased up. I had recurring symptoms, but not as severe as the ones I had on that Sunday morning. Three months later, the Saturday before Mother's Day, the inevitable happened. This time, there was no getting through or past it. I found myself in the emergency room with my LAD (widow maker) 100 percent blocked. Two of my RADs showed blockages. One was 99 percent blocked, and one was 79 percent blocked. Three stents and an extended stay in CCU later, I was home, recovering.

I know what you must be thinking: man, not only were you ignorant; you were in denial. You are absolutely right on both charges. Guilty! My ignorance was not bliss. It almost cost me my life. The reality is, I did not want to know what I already knew. I knew I was having heart issues, and I did not want to know.

I am just as amazed at how many Christians are living defeated lives and they know it, but they have no desire to do anything about it. Can you imagine what the Lord must be thinking? "And you shall *know the truth,* and the *truth shall make you free*" (John 8:32, NKJV; emphasis added). I would encourage you to read this verse over and over until the truth of it gets into your inner-most beings and becomes ineradicable. Jesus did not say that truth makes you free. He said the truth you know makes you free. Truth is truth whether you know it or not. Truth is truth whether you are free or not. It is truth you become intimate with that brings freedom.

When you know the truth about your new-creation identity in Christ is when you begin to live the kind of life you have always wanted to live.

Too Much Milk and Not Enough Meat—More Manna Please

The writer of the book of Hebrews is very straightforward in addressing the immaturity that existed in believers during the latter half of the first century. The following words would be appropriate for any gathering of believers to hear anywhere in the word today. "You have been believers so long now that you ought to be teaching others. Instead you need someone to teach you again the basic things about God's word. You are *like babies who need milk and cannot eat solid food.* For *someone who lives on milk is still an infant* and doesn't know how to do what is right. *Solid food is for those who are mature* who *through training* have the skill to recognize the difference between right and wrong" (Hebrews 5:12–14, NLT; emphasis added).

The writer did not say that milk was bad or that we ever outgrow our need for milk, but there does come a time when we must move on to solid food if we are to develop and mature as God designed. What is true in the natural realm is even more true in the spiritual realm. It is a healthy thing to hear the cries of newborn babies within the body of Christ. That is the sound of life being produced. But if we continue to feed people milk and never move them on to meat, they will never grow up and mature in their faith.

When our children were babies, we fed them milk or a milk formula. This was what they needed at the early stages of their growth to be healthy human beings. Later, we graduated them to baby food that came in jars. After that, we began to add "big people food" in very small portions in addition to their soft baby food. We would laugh and tell people, "Our little one sure is growing fast, eating table scraps now." This process continued until the child was able to eat just about anything by him- or herself. Our children would never have grown and matured into adults without the proper diet.

This same principle is true for the children of God. When we were born from above, we were babies in Christ. We need the milk of the word because the milk of the word tells us what happened when we accepted Christ. But then we needed to move on to "table scraps" and to the meat of the word. The meat of the word tells us who we are in Christ, our identities as His children. From there, we move to manna, which is Jesus Himself. This is when we begin discovering who we are in Christ and what Christ can and wants to do through us. The healthy diet for a child of God is milk, meat, and then manna. There will always be a need for milk in our Christian diets, but the time comes when meat must be added so we can become strong and healthy in our faith.

Once meat has become a steady part of our diets, we move to manna; that is feasting on Jesus and Jesus alone. We will always need the basics in our spiritual development, but nothing, absolutely nothing is more important than Jesus. Too many Christians are still in spiritual pampers and nursing on milk when they should be feeding others.

Jesus and His word are inseparable. "In the beginning was the Word, and the Word was with God, and the Word was God. And the Word became flesh and dwelt among us, and we beheld His glory, the glory as of the only begotten of the Father, full of grace and truth" (John 1:1, 14, NKJV). When we talk about feasting on manna (Jesus), we are not talking about excluding the written word of God; we are talking about including the living Word of God. According to 2 Timothy 3:16 (NKJV), the written word is the very breath of the living word.

What stunts our spiritual growth is thinking spiritual maturity is about information, when it is really all about transformation. Our heads can grow from being full of information while our spirits remain dwarfed from malnourishment.

In chapter six of the gospel of John, Jesus said that He was the bread of life. Then He said something strange. "Then Jesus said to them, 'Most assuredly, I say to you, unless you *eat the flesh of the Son of Man and drink His blood* you have no life in you'" (John 6:53, NKJV; emphasis added). Jesus says this several times in this passage of scripture in slightly different ways. He is certainly not talking about cannibalism as some charged Him with. He is talking about us being consumed by and with Him. He is the manna that came down from heaven, the only one who can quench thirst and satisfy a hungry soul. Jesus is our life, and when we feast on Him, we discover who we are in Him and what He can do through us.

When Jesus Becomes All We Want, We'll Have All We Need

When my oldest daughter was about five years old, she was learning the Twenty-Third Psalm along with her Sunday-morning bible class. A special Sunday had been designated for them to come into "big church" so they could proudly recite this beautiful Psalm to the entire church family. The big day finally arrived. As we were preparing to leave the house that morning, my daughter asked me if she could say the Twenty-Third Psalm to me. My heart was pounding with pride as I said, "You sure may." I will never forget how beautiful she looked as she began to rock back and forth on her heels and toes. She squared her shoulders, and with a big smile on her face, said, "The Lord is my Shepherd, *dat's* all I want." My five-year-old daughter may not have gotten the words quite right, but she nailed the heart of the Psalm. The Lord is my Shepherd; that is all I want. When He is all we want, we will find that He is all we need. When Jesus becomes all we want, we will be feasting on manna. This is the solid food the writer of Hebrews was talking about in chapter five.

Since we have been given a free will, it becomes our decision on how long we are without knowledge concerning our identities as children of God. Ignorance may be bliss in some areas, but certainly not when it comes to knowing who we are in Christ. We can know our identities if we want to know. It is a question of does our "want to," want to?

If we only knew that ignorance is not bliss when it comes to knowing who we are as new creations. What we do not know can and will hurt us.

19

If We Only Knew

You Can Never
Disappoint God

IN ALMOST FIFTY YEARS OF MINISTRY, I HAVE HEARD A LOT OF bizarre things said about God. Most of the things people say about God that are not true are not intended to impugn His character. We just repeat what we have heard, believing it is true. We cannot overstate the influence that these false statements have on our understanding of who God is.

There is an old axiom that says, if you say something for a long time, even though it may not be true, people will come to believe it. I heard some weird things growing up that I thought were true, when really, they were not. I believed some of those untruths even when I became an adult. I'll give you a few examples. When I was growing up, my parents would not allow us kids to drink milk when we ate fish. We were told that the combination of milk and fish created poison that would kill you. This scared the milk right out of us kids! To this day, I will not drink milk when I eat fish, and it is not because I believe it will kill me. I feel there are other drinks that go better with fish. Sweet tea is my personal choice. There is no scientific evidence that a mixture of fish and milk creates poison that will kill a person.

Here are a few of my mother's classic statements: If you go to bed with wet hair, you will wake up in the morning with a cold. Do not go outside with wet hair when it is cold, because you will catch pneumonia. Drinking coffee will turn your heels black. If you keep crossing your eyes, they will stick. Smoking will stunt your growth. If you use a brush instead of a comb when you comb your hair, you will not go bald. You need to wait at least an hour after eating before you go swimming. If you don't, you might get cramps and drown. Eating carrots will improve your eyesight. Time heals all wounds. Hopefully you get the point I am trying to make. Some of these sayings may have a scant of truth in them, but not enough to make them unequivocally true.

God Is Bigger Than Our Small Thinking

What we hear said about God will influence our thinking, affect our emotions, and shape our understanding of who God is to us. Here is one of the classic untruths that is said and believed about God. You need to be careful what you do, because you do not want to disappoint God. If you believe that it is possible to do something that will disappoint God, you will find it difficult to spend intimate time with Him. It will not be long before you begin to question His love for you. How can someone love you whom you have disappointed time and time again? The time will come when God becomes a distant deity in your mind. You may have a desire to come clean with Him, as if He does not know, but since you have disappointed Him so many times, you feel He is inaccessible, unapproachable, and unavailable to you.

The unadulterated truth is that you can never do anything that will ever disappoint God. God is so much bigger than our small thinking. It certainly is possible for us to grieve the Holy Spirit (Ephesians 4:30,

NKJV), quench the Holy Spirit (1 Thessalonians 5:19, NKJV), resist the Holy Spirit (Acts 7:51, NKJV), or insult the Holy Spirit (Hebrews 10:29, NKJV), but we can never disappoint God, even though we have been told we can.

Here is why. God is omniscient. That ten-letter word simply means He is all-knowing. There is absolutely nothing that is in our pasts, in our presents, or in our futures that God does not know. If it were possible for us to do something that God did not know we would do, then we could disappoint Him. Since that will never happen, we can never disappoint God. Never.

God Is the Master Chef

What about all the messes we have created for ourselves and for others through our bad behaviors, poor choices, and willful disobedience? What can God do with that? "And we know that all things work together for good to those who love God, to those who are the called according to His purpose" (Romans 8:28, NKJV). Paul is not saying that all things are good. He says that God has the ability to take all things and work them together for our good and for His glory.

Think about the talents and abilities that a good chef possesses. When a chef is preparing to bake a cake, on the counter, he or she will place all of the condiments that will be used in baking the cake. Each ingredient that will be used to make the cake may not taste good by itself. I do not think a mouthful of flour is that tasty. I have never seen a chef gulp down a teaspoon of salt by itself. A good chef can take all the ingredients, work them together, and have the end product be something that is awesome. Our God is the master chef. He has the ability to take everything that happens in our lives, even the bad that we have created by our poor choices, and work it all together for our good and for His glory.

By no means does this mean that we will never have to deal with the consequences of our poor choices. Some consequences may even be a lifetime companion. God can work anything and everything together to bring glory to Himself and make us better people. God will never be surprised or caught off guard by anything we do. Therefore, we can never disappoint Him.

God Does Not Think; He Knows

"Remember the things I have done in the past. For I alone am God! I am God, and there is none like Me. Only I can tell you the future before it happens. Everything I plan will come to pass, for I do whatever I wish" (Isaiah 46:9–10, NLT).

Pay close attention to what God says about Himself. It is absolutely stunning. He said that He alone is God, and there is none like Him. He knows what the future will be before the future ever becomes today. God never finds Himself in a spot where He has to have a committee meeting with His Son and the Holy Spirit to come up with a game plan. God does not think; He knows. Even when things in our lives seem to be falling apart, God is still in control. This is why we can trust Him with every aspect of our lives. He knows what is coming our way tomorrow.

When Jesus taught His disciples how to pray, He told them not to be like the hypocrites. They loved to pray long, repetitious prayers in public for show. He said, "Don't be like them, for *your Father knows exactly what you need even before you ask Him*" (Matthew 6:8, NLT; emphasis added). Our heavenly Father knows what we need before we even ask. This is where the confusion comes. When our prayers are not answered according to our requests, we assume that God did not answer our prayers at all. The truth is that what we are asking for may not be what we really need. We may think we know what our needs are, but God is the one who really knows. He even knows before we ask. Take Paul as an example. Paul had a thorn in his side, and three times he asked God to remove it. God knew that the presence of the thorn would produce in Paul what he really needed (2 Corinthians

12:7–9, NKJV). God did not remove the thorn, but He did give Paul an abundance of grace, which was his greatest need. Paul's preaching on God's amazing grace came out of the crucible of his own experience, not from something he had heard someone else say.

At the end of Genesis 3, it looks like God's experiment with humanity was a colossal failure. The only thing Adam and Eve did was what God told them not to do; they ate fruit from the tree of the knowledge of good and evil. Was this going to send God back to the drawing board? Would there be a redo?

Since God knows the future before it happens, Adam and Eve's disobedience did not surprise Him. Since He knew what they would do, He was not disappointed when they did it. The only way He could have been disappointed with them was if they had done something that He did not know they would do. We have an incredible heavenly Father.

When God escorted Adam and Eve from the garden, they went to work to provide for themselves, but He kept walking. What did He see that they could not see? "The Lamb who was slaughtered before the world was made" (Revelation 13:8, NLT). God had already taken care of the problem outside of time before there was ever a problem inside of time. God knew what reality was before reality ever was.

Peter's Wake Up Call

One of the most colorful characters in the New Testament is a man by the name of Simon Peter. He was one of the twelve disciples chosen by Jesus. Peter became the self-appointed spokesman for the dirty dozen. Someone once said that the only time Peter opened his mouth was to change feet. He always had one foot in his mouth. There is one thing for certain: Peter was never at a loss for words. Most people can tell you more about Peter's failure, his denial of Jesus, than they can tell you about the incredible sermon he preached on the day of Pentecost. This man did take a huge *step of unbelief*, but so did all of the disciples. This includes the beloved John. "Then they all forsook Him and fled" (Mark 14:50, NKJV). It wasn't just Peter who ran out on Jesus.

There was a moment when Peter stood head and shoulders above the crowd. Jesus knew that His disciples were hearing what people were saying about him on the streets. One day, when they were in the region of Caesarea Philippi, He asked His disciples what they were hearing. "Who do people think that I am?" (Matthew 16:13, NKKJV). They gave a litany of answers. Then Jesus served the ball into their court. "But who do you say that I am?" (Matthew 16:15, NKJV). Without hesitation, Peter piped up, "You are the Christ, the Son of the living God" (Matthew 16:16, NKJV). Kudos to Peter.

It would not be long before Peter's Spirit-empowered confession of the identity of Christ was exchanged for a denial of even knowing Him. He went from standing out from the crowd to trying to hide in the crowd. He got pointed out by a servant girl. When she put the spotlight on Peter as one of those who had been with Jesus, he denied it. A little while later, someone else exposed Peter as being one of those who had been with Jesus. Again, he denied it. An hour later, another individual with great confidence put his finger on Peter. For the third time, he denied even knowing who Jesus was. While the words of denial were rolling off his lips, the rooster crowed, "And the Lord turned and looked at Peter" (Luke 22:61, NKJV).

Can you imagine the emotions that must have flooded through Peter when Jesus turned and looked at him? The eye contact between them had to have been riveting. Like a clap of thunder, Peter had an instant recall of what Jesus had told him. "Peter, let me tell you something. Before the rooster crows tomorrow morning, you will deny three times that you even know me" (Luke 22:34, NLT).

Was Jesus disappointed in Peter? Absolutely not. For Jesus to be disappointed, Peter would have had to do something that Jesus did not expect him to do. Jesus had prophesied Peter's denial. God knew reality before it was real. God used the rooster's crow as an alarm clock to wake Peter up.

When Jesus turned and looked at Peter, it was not with a look of anger or disappointment. It was Jesus's way of saying, "I still love you Peter. You will be OK." "Peter went out and wept bitterly" (Luke 22:62, NKJV). When we do and say things that are not in keeping with our identities as believers and we know that we are stilled loved unconditionally by our heavenly Father, it is a game changer. Because God is all-knowing, we can never do anything that He did not know we would do. Therefore, we can never disappoint God. This creates in us a desire not to do things that are not in keeping with who we are as new creations. Knowing we cannot disappoint God does not lead to rebellion. It leads to obedience.

God Knows Everything about Everything

Since God has full knowledge about everything, then nothing can ever happen that surprises Him. Since God cannot be surprised or caught off guard, He cannot be disappointed. Because God is all-knowing, He even knows the future before it happens. God told Jeremiah that He knew him before he was in his mother's womb (Jeremiah 1:5, NKJV). The Psalmist David said that God knew us before we were ever born. Not only did God have every day of our lies recorded in His book before our days of birth; He had every moment of every day laid out before a single day had passed (Psalms 139:16, NKJV). Nothing, and I mean absolutely nothing, happens in our lives that takes God by surprise. Since God will never be surprised by anything we do, He will never be disappointed by anything we do. We may disappoint ourselves when we do not live up to our potential, but we will never disappoint God.

God does not think the way we do. He just knows. He does not have to go through a thinking process to form an opinion about anything. He already has His opinion. What He thinks is the way it is, too. God does not have to bring His thoughts in line with our thoughts. We must bring our thoughts in line with His. "'My thoughts are not your thoughts, Nor are your ways My ways,' says the Lord. 'For as the heavens are higher than the earth, So are My ways higher than your ways, And My thoughts than your thoughts'" (Isaiah 55:9–10, NKJV).

Since we do not have full knowledge about anything, then what we think is based on what we know. That means our thinking is constantly changing, because the information we have about something or someone is always increasing. Our thoughts about most things are constantly in flux.

To think is to have an opinion or idea about something. When someone or something does not live up to our expectations and hopes, we can be disappointed. When our hopes and expectations are not satisfied, we can find ourselves unhappy and discouraged. Disappointment comes because our hopes and expectations are not fulfilled. What we expected did not happen.

Since God possesses full knowledge about everything, His thoughts never change. This is why His thoughts are not our thoughts. Our thinking is always being aligned with reality. God's thoughts are reality.

Paul addresses the subject of our thought-lives in his second letter to the Corinthians. We are to take all our thoughts captive, to the obedience of Christ (2 Corinthians 10:5, NKJV). That simply means that we are to teach our thoughts to be obedient to Christ and to His thoughts. We are to think about things the way Christ thinks about them. We need to see things the way He sees them. His thoughts never change about anything, because thoughts are based on knowledge. God is all-knowing, so His thoughts are reality. What God said about something in the beginning is still true today. What was reality then is reality today. Whatever God says is reality for all of time and eternity.

"For, who can know the Lord's thoughts? Who knows enough to teach Him? But we understand these things, for *we have the mind of Christ*" (1 Corinthians 2:16, NLT; italics added).

If we only knew that the exchanged life is what makes it possible for us to think about things the way God thinks about things. Our minds were exchanged for His mind when we had our born-from-above experiences. His thoughts can now be our thoughts, and His ways should be our ways.

If We Only Knew
We Were Worth Saving

I WOULD SUGGEST THAT YOU READ THE TITLE OF THIS CHAPTER one more time. It does not say what you may think it says. It does not say that we were *worthy* to be saved. It says we were *worth saving*. There is a difference. We certainly were not worthy to be saved, for there was nothing good in us that made us worthy. "As the scriptures say, no one is righteous—not even one" (Romans 3:10, NLT). That has the ring of inclusion. Do you think that when the scriptures say no one is righteous, it actually means no one?

Even though we were not worthy to be saved, God saw that we were worth saving. If we are worth saving, then we are worth providing for. Some may think that drawing a distinction between the words *worth* and *worthy* is quibbling over something that is inconsequential. To that, I would say, not understanding the difference between the two words can have a consequential impact on understanding why we were accepted by God.

Both words, *worth* and *worthy*, can be used as nouns or as adjectives. When the word *worth* is used in either case, it refers to value. On the other hand, when the word *worthy* is used as an adjective, it is usually followed by the preposition *of*. It describes something or someone having qualities that deserve recognition. When God looked at humankind, He saw nothing that was deserving of recognition. If God cannot see something, it cannot be seen. There was a moment in time when the depravity of the human race evoked this response from God: "The Lord observed the extent of human wickedness on the earth, and he saw that everything they thought or imagined was consistently and totally evil. So the Lord was sorry he had ever made them and put them on the earth. It broke is heart" (Genesis 6:5–6, NLT).

When God looked at us, He did not see us worthy of being saved. There was nothing in us that attracted Him. It was His love that drew Him to us. He saw us as worth saving. Since we are worth saving, we are worth providing for.

Our Unworthiness Makes God Approachable

"I'm not sure God will accept me. You don't know what I've done. I feel so unworthy." Do these statements sound familiar? They should, because it is said by people all the time who are keenly aware of their *unworthiness*. How can someone who is so unholy approach God, who is not only holy, but thrice holy (Isaiah 6:3, NKJV)? The truth is, the only reason we can approach God is because of our unworthiness. It is our unworthiness that causes us to see our need. God is the only one who can take what is unworthy and make it worthy. He can take what is unfit and make it fit. When we come to the Lord, in essence we are saying, "Lord, there is nothing in me that is deserving of your love and acceptance. You are my only hope. There is nothing in me that is deserving of your presence. I am coming to you because I am unworthy." It is our unworthiness that makes God approachable. Our goodness is not what attracts the Lord; it is His love for us.

When we see God's holiness, we become keenly aware of our unworthiness. What brought Isaiah to the point of saying, "Woe is me, for I am undone! Because I am a man of unclean lips, And I dwell in the midst of a people of unclean lips" (Isaiah 6:5, NKJV)? During a time of great pain, Isaiah saw God, high and lifted up, sitting on His throne in all of His glory. The entire heavenly realm shook from the thundering voices of the angels as they flew around God's throne, singing, "Holy, holy, holy" (Isaiah 6:3, NJV). The moment Isaiah saw God's holiness, he became instantly aware of his unworthiness. When God revealed His holiness, Isaiah immediately saw his need: "It's all over, I am doomed, for I am a sinful man, I have filthy lips, and I live among people with filthy lips, Yet I have seen the king, the Lord of heaven's armies" (Isaiah 6:4, NLT). When Isaiah saw the holiness of God, he was overwhelmed by his unworthiness.

Any attempt to compare humanity's goodness to the holiness of God is like comparing a thimbleful of water to the Atlantic Ocean. It would be ludicrous to make such a comparison. If you want to see how imperfect you are, measure yourself by perfection. God's perfection will magnify our imperfection.

Good works will never be the reason anyone is ever declared righteous before God. Our justifications, our legal standing before God, will never be because God saw so much good in us that He just had to accept us. The word of God says that there is none righteous, not even one. Adam's fall affected us all. He passed on his sinful seed to all of humanity—total depravity. The doctrine of total depravity asserts that because of the fall, it is impossible for people to love God with their whole hearts, minds, and strength. Humanity, by nature, is inclined to serve its own desires and will. God's rule of government is rejected.

Our Worth Comes from God

God is all-seeing. There is nothing, and I mean absolutely nothing, that is hidden from His sight. "Nothing in all creation is hidden from God. Everything is naked and exposed before his eyes, and he is the one to whom we are accountable" (Hebrews 4:13, NLT). Since nothing is hidden from His view, that means secret sin on earth is an open scandal in heaven. He sees it all. Since God sees everything, He not only sees our unworthiness; He sees our worth. He saw that we were worth saving.

It was not humanity's goodness that attracted God; it was His love for humanity, even when humanity did not want anything to do with Him. "But God demonstrates His own love toward us, in that while we were still sinners, Christ died for us" (Romans 5:8, NKJV). God's grace is amazing! God put on public display His love for fallen humanity by sending Christ to die on a cross, not for the godly, but for the ungodly. Why would He do that? He saw that we were worth saving. He sees in us what we cannot see in ourselves. He is constantly calling out of us what He put in us. In Psalms 139, David says that God knew us when we were being formed in the secret place of our mother's wombs. How could God watch us while we were being formed? He is all-seeing. There is nothing hidden from His sight. God sees the worth that He weaved in us while we were still in the secret place. David boldly declares that we were fearfully and wonderfully made.

If you want to see how a child starts to get his or her sense of worth, watch a young mother interacting with her firstborn child. It is a sight to behold. The baby that is being loved on has no clue as to its self-worth. How could it? The child just came out of the secret place. The mother tells the infant how special he or she is. "You're so precious. Yes you are." "You are a cutie pie." "You are a special gift from heaven. Mommy sure loves you. Yes she does." The cuddling and cooing that goes on between a mother and her baby is very special. What is this young mother doing? She is confirming to the child its worth before the child is even aware that it has a need to know. The worth of every individual that has ever been born was placed in them by the Creator, while each was being formed in the secret place.

Our heavenly Father wants all His children to know that they have worth and that they are valuable to the Lord. You were worth saving. Because you are worth saving, you are worth providing for. He loves you more than you will ever know. God's opinion of us is incredibly important. Our happiness in life depends on how we think God sees and feels about us. If we have unhealthy opinions about how God feels about us, it will affect our abilities to live successful lives of faith. How can you trust someone when you are not sure if he or she really loves you or not? When we see ourselves the way God sees us, it can change our entire perspectives on life. We can live in contentment, a state of happiness and satisfaction, when we know that we are extremely and wonderfully loved by our heavenly Father. It does not matter how old we get, either. It is important for us to know that we are children of God and that He is madly in love with us (Romans 8:17, NKJV).

Worth Saving, Worth Providing For

"Now you are no longer a slave but God's own child. And since you are his child, God has made you His heir" (Galatians 4:7, NLT). You are not a slave, a stranger, or an orphan. You may feel like you are at times, but we know that truth is not based on our feelings. Even though feelings are real, they may not be true. Once you have been born into God's family, you are His child, regardless of how you may feel at times. Feelings are always in a state of flux. On the other hand, truth is truth no matter what. The word of God is truth.

Since you are in God's family by birth, that makes you a child of God. Now that you are His child, He has made you an heir. An heir of God! Let that stir in your innermost being for a while. To know that you are in God's family and that everything He has is yours, is not pride or vanity or being self-righteous. It is the truth, supported by the word of God. "For all who are led by the Spirit of God are children of God. So you have not received a spirit that makes you fearful slaves. Instead, you received God's Spirit when he adopted you as his own children. *Now we call him, Abba, Father.* For his Spirit joins with our spirit to affirm that we are God's children. And since we are God's children, we are his heirs. In fact, together with Christ we are heirs of

God's glory. But if we share his glory, we must also share his suffering" (Romans 8:14–17, NLT; italics added).

As trusting children, we can expect our heavenly Father to protect us, to provide for us, and to care for us. "And my God shall supply all your need according to His riches in glory by Christ Jesus" (Philippians 4:18, NKJV). I know what some people are thinking. Yes, there are times when things do not turn out the way we were hoping and praying they would. When that happens, it does not mean that God did not hear and answer our prayers. Sometimes, the best thing for us can be when God seems to remain silent. In times of silence, God may be giving us time to rethink our thinking. God does say no, and at other times, He may say to wait. We do get disappointed when things do not turn out according to our expectations. That is why it is so important for us to trust our heavenly Father. Father knows best.

When I first began preaching many years ago, I preached at nursing homes, in bible classes, at special gatherings, at homecomings, on Memorial Day, and occasionally, in a local church. It really did not matter where I preached, just so long as I got to preach. There came a time when I got the itch to pastor a local church. I thought I was ready since I had been preaching for two years or so. During this pastor-itch season I was in, a local church where I had preached a few times was looking for a pastor. After praying about it for a few minutes, I just knew I was their guy. They knew me, and I thought I knew them. To make a sad story even sadder, they called someone else. Oh yes, they did. Even though this happened over fifty-years ago, I can still remember the feelings of rejection that I had. Of course, I never shared these feelings of rejections and hurt with anyone. What would that make me look like?

During the next two years, this church, where I just knew I was their man, went through three pastors. All three were good men too. If I had gotten what I had asked for, I am not sure I would still be in the ministry today. I was so young and inexperienced that if I had gotten what I thought I was ready for, it could have destroyed me and my ministry. To make this sad story glad, a short while after that, a little country church asked me to come and be their pastor. That was an incredible experience, and I learned so much. These were some of the sweetest people on the planet. I was treated more like their grandson than a pastor. They put up with some horrible preaching. Since most of them were hard of hearing, I survived.

Getting what we ask for may not be what we really need. Our heavenly Father is all-knowing. Since He knows everything, He knows what our real needs are. He knows what will help us or hurt us; He knows what we are ready for and what we are not ready for. He can be trusted. "Every good gift and every perfect gift is from above, and comes down from the Father of lights, with whom there is no variation or shadow of turning" (James 1:17, NKJV). Since He saw that we were worth saving, we are worth providing for. He is a good, good Father.

What Happened to Our Unworthiness?

Unworthiness is a debilitating emotion. Feelings of unworthiness can be very painful. It is a weapon the enemy uses very skillfully to discourage and defeat God's children. This is why it is so important to understand that our born-from-above experiences were an exchange, not a change. God did not take the old people we were and make those people better, cleaner, and acceptable. God is not into renovating anything. He is all about creating. When we said yes to Jesus Christ as our Lord and Savior, at that very moment, the people we were, were exchanged for completely new people. There was an exchange of what was unworthy for something that is worthy. The new creation not only has worth; it is worthy.

When you meet a believer who has discovered who Christ has made them to be, you may think he or she is conceited when actually, the person is convinced. The believer who is convinced of his or her identity in Christ knows he or she is a peculiar person. From the bible's perspective, being peculiar does not mean a person is weird, odd, or strange. Being peculiar means belonging to the king, the king's spoils.

After a great victory in war, the king's army would go through the battlefield and mark certain items as belonging to the king. These spoils-of-war were marked *peculiar*. They were special and became a part of the king's treasury.

As a child of the king, you have been marked peculiar. You belong to the King of kings. You are a part of His treasured family. Now that you belong to the king, you are of great worth. Because you are His, your unworthiness has been exchanged for His worthiness.

What do we do with our feelings of not being holy enough? Always submit your feelings to the truth. The word of God is truth. As a child of God, you are holy because you have been consecrated, set apart for God (John 17:14–16, NKJV). You have been marked as being peculiar. You do not have to worry about being holy enough, because Jesus was perfectly holy when He went to the cross on your behalf. It has nothing to do with what we can do for Him; it is all about what He has done for us. We did not do anything for God to accept us, and we cannot do anything for God to reject us. I love what someone said, "We can't lose with our bad works what we did not get with our good works." Jesus did not do anything to be made sin, and we did not do anything to be made righteous. "Not by works of righteousness which we have done, but according to His mercy He saved us, through the washing of regeneration and renewing of the Holy Spirit, whom He poured out on us abundantly through Jesus Christ our Savior" (Titus 3:5–6, NKJV).

God's Heart Is Always Set on Us

"I will never fail you. I will never abandon you" (Hebrews 13:5, NLT). The writer of Hebrews is quoting from the book of Deuteronomy. They are taking a small snippet from Israel's history to emphasize the faithfulness of God. Israel is on the verge of crossing over the Jordan River into the land of promise. The leadership rod is being passed from Moses to Joshua. In his address to all of Israel,

Moses tells them that he would not be crossing over the Jordan with them. Joshua would be their new leader. Moses tells them not to worry, because God would go before them like He always had. He told them to be strong and of good courage. Then Moses says this about God— not once, but twice: "He will not leave you nor forsake you; do not fear nor be dismayed" (Deuteronomy 31:8, NKJV).

We have been given the same promise. God is always with us, because He dwells within us, in the person of the Holy Spirit. He does not come and go. He has made His home in us. We can be strong and take courage by knowing this. The Hebrews 13 passage tells us that God's heart is always set on us. That means He loves us when we are lovable, and He loves us when we are unlovable. God loved us yesterday when we were behaving right, and He loves us today when we are not behaving right. God's love for us is not predicated by what we do or what we do not do. He never changes; God is love (1 John 4:8, NKJV). Our misbehaviors do not change Him or the love that He has for us.

One Man's Trash Is God's Treasure

The concept of something having contradictory qualities to different people has been around for a long time. What one person may consider worthless, may be highly prized or valued by someone else—or even by several people. Humanity has the tendency to compare people with people. When someone does not measure up to our standards, our tendencies are to think less of them. The word of God has some strong words when it comes to comparing people with people. "Oh, don't worry; we wouldn't dare say that we are as wonderful as these other men who tell you how important they are! But they are only comparing themselves with each other, using themselves as the standard of measurement. How ignorant" (2 Corinthians 10:12, NLT)!

After almost fifty years as a pastor of local churches, I have seen some interesting people. There is one individual who is at the top of my list. I will call him James Henry Taylor. This man just may be the most unique person I have ever pastored. God used him to teach me so much about the value of one person.

James Henry Taylor was a hard worker, a loyal church member, a generous giver, and a lover of God. I do not think I have ever been around anyone who loved God more than James Henry Taylor. Not only did he love the Lord, but he was not intimidated whatsoever by sharing his love for the Lord with anyone, anywhere. If he passed the church's facilities and saw vehicles in the parking lot, he joined in on the meeting. It did not matter if it was a lady's group, a youth conference, a baby shower, or a staff-leadership meeting, James Henry Taylor was there! It was his church family, and he felt he had the right to be a part of whatever was going on.

The job that James Henry Taylor did for a living was very hard. What he did at work could not be done without getting dirty—sometimes very dirty. Because he did not practice good personal hygiene, it often created a little tension in a group setting. Especially if it was a small group. No one in the church family was ever rude to James Henry to my knowledge, but you could tell some were uncomfortable with the aroma that he emitted at times. OK, most of us were uncomfortable.

At the end of every service, without fail, James Henry Taylor would seek me out to give me some keen insight into what I had just ministered on. He thought the way a young child thinks, and what he shared with me usually made sense. When he talked, you had to listen carefully because he was hard to understand. To make things more challenging, James Henry would get two inches away from your nose when he talked to you. To keep from being overwhelmed by his bad breath, I would cuff my hand over my mouth in a way so I could smell the cologne on my hand as we talked. Walking down the hallway one Sunday, after one of our conversations, I said out loud, "Lord, you have to do something with James Henry Taylor." The Lord's response to me was immediate. "Wayne, you're my James Henry Taylor." I learned more about the value of one person from that one simple statement from the Lord than I have learned in my entire life. The Lord gave me a glimpse of how He sees an individual. To Him, every person has worth and is valuable. I also learned a lot about what was in my heart.

To God, everyone is worth saving. "For *God so loved the world* that He gave His only begotten Son, that *whoever believes in Him* should not perish but have everlasting life" (John 3:16, NKJV; italics added). Everyone is worth saving, or Jesus would not have died for the world. It is not a matter of someone having enough good qualities for God to receive him or her into His family; it is about the goodness of God. It has nothing to do with our worthiness; it is about whosoever believes or trusts *in* Him. "For God does not show favoritism" (Romans 2:11, NLT).

If we only knew that we are worth saving. Since we are worth saving, we are worth providing for. It is not about how good we are; it is about how good God is. Whatever God is, He is completely. Since He is good, He is completely good.

21

If We Only Knew
Death Is Dead to a Believer

IT WAS A GOOD DAY WHEN I WAS RELEASED FROM THE MILITARY hospital and sent home for a thirty-day leave of absence before reporting to Fort Bragg, North Carolina. I spent several months in the hospital recovering from wounds I received in Vietnam. It felt so good to be home, where I could hear the familiar voices of my family and friends, smell my mother's good cooking, and sleep in a comfortable bed—not to mention being able to take a shower whenever I wanted. I was on the verge of getting comfortable being home when the phone rang and my mother asked me if I would answer it. When I said hello, the voice on the other end of the line said, "Who is this?" Of course, my response was, "This is Wayne." I wasn't ready for what this person said next: "I thought you were dead." There was a moment of awkward silence before I responded with, "I'm sorry to disappoint you."

This individual was not trying to be mean or insensitive to me or my situation with that statement. It was an elderly friend of my mother whose information about me being wounded in Vietnam was still sketchy. The first report my mother received was that I was missing in action. You can imagine how upset that made her. A few days later, she received another report saying that I had been wounded and was in the hospital in Japan. My mother was told that the government would make arrangements for her to talk to me by phone as soon as possible. That was one of the best phone calls I have every received.

Many of my buddies were not as fortunate as I had been. The lyrics in the song "Some Gave All" by Billy Ray Cyrus are apropos: "All gave some, some gave all." I gave some, but so many of my buddies gave all. They are the true heroes, and I salute them to this day.

The First Discussion of Death

Death is not a subject that most people enjoy talking about, yet God talked to Adam about it before sin ever entered the human race. I deal with the first mention of death in chapter 4 of my book, "The Scam." I will give you a short recapitulation of it.

God had a conversation with Adam at the very beginning of time, and He talked to him about death. I will paraphrase what God said to Adam about death. "The day you eat from the tree of the knowledge of good and evil, *you will die*" (Genesis 2:17, NKJV; personal paraphrase). This raises a legitimate question. Who created death? Where did death come from? Without thinking, most people say that death came from the devil and that he is the one who created death. There is one huge problem with that answer. The created cannot create. The devil is a created being; therefore, he cannot create. That reduces our choices considerably. Since there is only one Creator, God had to be the one who created death.

When God looked at all he had created, He said it was *"very good"* (Genesis 1:31, NKJV; emphasis added). What in the world is good about death? I will tell you what is good about death: when it is lifeless. When death has no power. God created death with no life. Before you get upset with God about creating death, you may want to think your way through it. God is the one who informed Adam about death. I would say this was an act of love. God told Adam that death had no

If We Only Knew

power whatsoever as long as he was obedient. We know from Genesis 3 that Adam was disobedient to God's word. Adam's disobedience gave birth to sin, and sin gave life to death. His choice to disobey God activated death.

God did not kill Adam for his disobedience; death did. Death did not decide one day that it would come alive and kill Adam. Adam chose to be killed by death when he chose to disobey God. "Through one man sin entered the world, and *death through sin*, and thus *death spread to all men*, because all sinned" (Romans 5:12, NKJV; emphasis added). Humanity's sin gave life and power to death. *Death through sin* tells us that death did not come through Adam the man. Death came through Adam's act of disobedience. Adam's sin gave life to death, and death took life from humanity.

The only way God could put death back to sleep again was to destroy sin. "He [God] made Him [Jesus] who knew no sin to be sin for us, that we might become the righteousness of God in Him" (2 Corinthians 5:21, NKJV). The reason Jesus came to the earth was to destroy the curse of death. Jesus came to put death back to sleep. His death took life out of death. His resurrection put life into the dead. He was made into what I was so I could be what He is. We can also say it this way: What I was, He was made into so that what He is, I became. "So death, tell me, where is your victory? Tell me death, where is your sting? It is sin that gives death its sting and the law that gives sin its power" (1 Corinthians 15:55, TPT). As children of God, death has no claim on us. Death is dead to a believer.

One Foot in Faith, One Foot in Unbelief

Jesus had gotten word from Mary and Martha that their brother, Lazarus, was sick. After hearing this news, Jesus stayed where He was for two more days. When Jesus finally arrived in Bethany, He was told that Lazarus had died and had been in the tomb for four days. When Martha heard that Jesus had come, she ran out to meet Him. The first words that came out of her mouth were, "Lord, if you had come when we sent you word that our brother was sick, Lazarus would still be alive" (John 11:21, NKJV). "You were only two miles away." Jesus told Martha that her brother would rise again (John 11:23, NKJV). Her response was, "I know that he will rise again in the resurrection at the last day" (John 11:24, NKJV). Pay close attention to what Jesus said to Martha in response to what she said. "I am the resurrection and the life. He who believes in Me, though he may die, he shall live. And whoever lives and believes in Me shall never die. *Do you believe this?*" (John 11:25, NKJV; emphasis added). Martha said that she believed her brother would rise again. She now had one foot planted in faith: I believe my brother will rise again.

When Jesus told them to remove the stone that had been placed over the mouth of the tomb, it was Martha who said, "Lord, he has been dead for four days. The smell will be horrible" (John 11:39, NLT). This is the same Martha who just said she believed her brother would rise from the dead. With that statement, she planted her other foot in unbelief. Martha had one foot planted in verse 27 (NLT), faith, and one foot planted in verse 39 (NLT), unbelief. Martha's *foot of unbelief* planted in verse 39 negates her *foot of belief* planted in verse 27. Does this have a familiar ring to it? It should, because Martha's story could be our stories. All of us have had those moments when it appears that we have one foot planted in faith and one foot planted in unbelief. When that happens, we are actually saying that we really do not believe, because there is no middle ground between the two. We either believe, or we do not believe. It is possible to vacillate between the two.

James warns us about wavering between faith and unbelief. "If you need wisdom, ask our generous God, and He will give it to you. He will not rebuke you for asking. But when you ask him, *be sure that your faith is in God alone. Do not waver,* for a person with divided loyalty is as unsettled as a wave of the sea that is blown and tossed by the wind. Such people should not expect to receive anything from the Lord. Their loyalty is divided between God and the world, and they are unstable in everything they do" (James 1:5–8, NLT; emphasis added). Allow me to sum up what James said on one sentence: Make sure you have both feet planted in Christ and in Christ alone.

Precious in the Sight of the Lord

If you have children, I am sure you have some precious memories of their firsts—the first time to turn over in their cribs, their first times to crawl, their first step(s), their first words. Those moments are precious and are forever etched into our memories. The Psalmist reveals something that is precious to our Lord. It might be a little surprising to some people what God considers precious. "Precious in the sight of the Lord is the death of His saints" (Psalms 116:15, NKJV). Why would the death of a child of God be precious in the sight of the Lord? Could it be because He knows something about death that we do not know? I would think that is a safe bet.

In writing his second letter to the church at Corinth, Paul talks about the death of a child of God. "We are confident, yes, well pleased rather to be absent from the body and to be present with the Lord" (2 Corinthians 5:8, NKJV). To be absent from our bodies and to be in the Lord's presence is a much better life. When we die, we do not cease to exist, and we do not spend time in a *holding area* before we make our final arrivals into God's presence: We are absent, and then we are present.

In his letter to the Philippians, Paul also talked about death. He told his spiritual family that he was caught between a rock and a hard place, between living and dying. "For I am hard-pressed *between the two*, having a desire *to depart* and be with Christ, which is far better. Nevertheless *to remain* in the flesh is more needful for you" (Philippians 1:23–24, NKJV; emphasis added). Paul knew that it would be better for the people if he continued to live. Death would be better for him because he would be ushered into the presence of the Lord. To be absent from the body is to be present with the Lord.

The reason most Christians are not comfortable with the subject of death is because we do not know what happened to death when Jesus died. Go back and read the section in this chapter on the first discussion of death that God had with Adam. When Jesus died, death died. When Jesus died, life was taken out of death. Before we had our born-from-above experiences, we were spiritually dead. When Jesus arose from the dead, He gave life to the dead. As children of God, death has no power as far as we are concerned. For us, death has no sting, and the grave has no victory (2 Corinthians 15:55, NKJV).

When you see the word *death* used in relationship with a child of God, it carries with it the meaning of folding a tent, falling asleep, or weighing anchor. There is nothing dreadful about falling asleep when you are exhausted or folding up a tent after a camping trip. My favorite is weighing an anchor. Think about a ship that is moored to a dock. When it is time to set sail, the captain will weigh the anchor, lifting it off the sea floor and hoisting it up to be stored aboard the ship. Once the anchor is secured aboard, the ship is moved away from the dock, and it begins its journey.

If you stand and watch a ship long enough after it has departed the port, it will soon pass over the horizon and out of physical sight. The ship does not cease to exist; it is now in a position where it cannot be seen. That is how Paul describes death for a believer. We do not cease to exist; we just move into a realm that cannot be seen by physical eyes. To be absent from our bodies is to be present with our Lord.

We Don't Grieve as Those Who Have No Hope

I find it very interesting that most believers are ignorant of the very thing that God does not want us to be ignorant about. "I don't want you to be ignorant brethren, concerning *those who have fallen asleep*, lest you sorry as others who have no hope" (1 Thessalonians 4:13, NKJV; emphasis added). Paul uses the expression *falling asleep* in this passage to describe death for a child of God.

Paul also addresses the subject of grieving over the death of a loved one in this verse. He does not say that a believer should never grieve when a loved one dies. That would not be a fair expectation. When you love, you grieve. But a child of God has hope so he or she does not grieve like those who have no hope. Our hope comes from knowing that Christ's death took life out of death for us. For us, death has no sting, and the grave has no victory. Death is only the vehicle that carries us into our heavenly Father's presence.

Paul ends his short teaching on death for a child of God and the return of Christ with these words: "Therefore *comfort* one another with these words" (1 Thessalonians 4:18, NKJV; emphasis added). The word *comfort* means to strengthen, to fortify, to make strong, to give courage. That sounds like the ministry of the Holy Spirit, doesn't it?

When Death Comes Knocking

The day will come when death makes a personal visit and knocks on your door. Death does not discriminate on the basis of age. When a person is born, he or she is old enough to die. The bible says that every person is destined to die (Hebrews 9:27, NLT). Death comes once per person.

When you accepted God's gift of life and received Jesus as your Lord and Savior, death lost its claim on you.

> Then I saw a new heaven and a new earth, for the first heaven and the old earth had disappeared. And the sea was also gone. And I saw the holy city, the new Jerusalem, coming down from God out of heaven like a bride beautifully dressed for her husband. I heard a loud voice shout from the throne, saying, "Look, God's home is now among his people! He will live with them, and they will be his people.

God himself will be with them. He will wipe every
tear from their eyes and *there will be no more death
or sorrow or dying or pain*. All these things are gone
forever" (Revelation 21:1–4, NLT; emphasis added).

If we only knew that death has no life to us as believers, then we
could start living.

If We Only Knew

The Deep State Every Child
of God Has to Deal With

WE CAN BE OUR OWN WORST ENEMIES AT TIMES AND BE TOTALLY
oblivious to it. It is possible to be convinced that we are fighting the
enemy when we are actually fighting ourselves. As the saying goes,
"Make sure your worst enemy is not living between your own two
ears" (Laird Hamilton). Too many Christians are allowing the enemy
to live in their heads rent free, and the enemy's voice has become as
familiar as a family member's. The strongest muscles we possess and
also our worst enemies can be our minds.

It has been said that the first reaction to truth that challenges our
preconceived ideas is usually a negative one. There will be some sort
of pushback from within when we are told that what we believe about
something is not supported by the scriptures. I find this to be true
in my own life. Our humanity likes comfort, and we can get a little
annoyed when our comfort zones are encroached upon, especially if
some of our pet peeves are threatened. The ones I have in mind in this
chapter are our identities as new creations in Christ.

Even though truth never changes, our understanding of truth is always changing. What truth was yesterday, truth will be today, and it will be truth tomorrow—because it is truth. On the other hand, our understanding of truth is constantly expanding as we mature in our faith and comprehension of our new-creation identities. This maturation process will not go unchallenged by the deep state operatives that live within us. The deep state within us will always try to pervert the legitimacy of our true identities as believers through manipulation and control.

There are three deep-state actors that constantly challenge our spiritual growth process and seek to overthrow our identities as believers. I call them the Big Three: Our thoughts, our feelings, and our experiences. Because thoughts, feelings, and experiences are real, we assume they are always true. It has never dawned on most believers that just because something is real does not mean it is true. We can feel that God does not love us. These feelings are real, but they are certainly not true. God is love, and nothing will ever cause Him to not love us. The writer of Hebrews says that God will never turn His heart from us (Hebrews 13:5, NKJV). That means that since He loved us yesterday when we were loveable, He will love us today when we are unlovable. "For I am the Lord, I do not change" (Malachi 3:6, NKJV).

We are ever-learning, and that is a good thing, even though it can leave us in a conundrum at times. Our understanding of truth comes from revelation by the Holy Spirit. This is why He is called the Spirit of Truth (John 14:16–17, NKJV). The Spirit of Truth dwells with and abides in every believer. Simply stated, the Holy Spirit is Christ's continual presence in us. "However, when He, the Spirit of truth has come, He will guide you into all truth; for He will not speak on His own authority, but whatever He hears He will speak; and He will tell you things to come. He will glorify Me, for He will take of what is Mine and declare it to you. All things that the Father has are Mine. Therefore I said that He will take of Mine and declare it to you" (John 16:13–15, NKJV). The Spirit of God knows everything about everything and has promised to teach us all things. How good is that?

The Spirit of Truth will continually fill the hearts of the hungry with good things (Luke 1:53, NKJV). It does not matter how good the food may be or how well it is served; nothing sounds good if we are not hungry. Those who are hungry are the ones God fills with good things.

The Deep State Exposed

We were not created as spiritual robots, incapable of thinking and feeling. Life would be very mechanical without the Big Three. The unique ability to think and to feel were hardwired in us at conception. It is one of the many things that set us apart from other life-forms.

What a person thinks and how a person feels is very personal. We do a great disservice if we tell someone that his or her thoughts and feelings are not real. After all, God created us with the ability to think and to feel. But what people do need to know is, the Big Three were never intended by our Creator to be the judge for what is true and what is not true. Our thoughts and feelings are too capricious to be trusted with that sacred assignment. The standard of truth has been and will always be the word of God. "Make them holy by your truth; teach them *your word, which is truth*" (John 17:17, NLT; emphasis added). The unchangeable word of God is our standard for truth. Whatever the word of God says is what we need to embrace as truth; even if it goes against what we have thought, felt, and have believed. We must always bring our thoughts, feelings, and our experiences in line with the word of God. There are times when we can trust our feelings, but we should never allow our feelings to be the judge for what is true. If we ever allow our feelings to become the litmus test for what is true, we are setting ourselves up for certain defeat.

The Big Three are what the enemy uses in his attempt to pull off a spiritual coup. The devil can never undo what Christ has done in you, but he can distort your understanding of what Christ did for you by getting you to rely on your thoughts, feelings, and experiences to define your identity as a child of God. I am not saying that our thoughts, feelings, and experiences are always wrong, but I am saying that we should never allow the Big Three to determine and define what is spiritually true and what is not true, because they are ever-changing.

Who are you as a new creation in Christ? The word of God says, "Anyone who belongs to Christ has become a new person. The old life is gone; a new life has begun" (2 Corinthians 5:17, NLT). What do these words mean to you? Do you belong to Christ? If so, you are a new person. Your old life is gone, and your new life has begun. You were a sinner in your old life. You are a saint in your new life. Following on the heels of Paul's testimony in Romans 7 about his life before Christ, he writes in the very next chapter, "So then those who are in the flesh cannot please God. *But you are not in the flesh but in the Spirit*, if indeed the Spirit of God dwells in you. Now if anyone does not have the Spirit of Christ, he is not His" (Romans 8:8–9, NKJV; emphasis added).

The devil's nefarious scheme is to steal the identity of every child of God so he or she cannot enjoy his or her birthright privileges. He uses our thoughts, our feelings, and our experiences to accomplish this goal. There are many examples I could use that are believed by the evangelical community to prove this point. In my opinion, a believer's identity is the number-one target of the enemy's coup attempt. He has had great success in convincing many believers within the community of faith that as children of God, we are only sinners saved by grace.

For more years than I would like to admit, this was my position as to my identity as a child of God. I saw and identified myself as a sinner saved by grace. When you think about it, this statement has all the signs of legitimacy. I am saved and I do sin, so it stands to reason I am a sinner saved by grace. This position squares with my thoughts, with my feelings, and with my experiences; therefore, it must be true. What exacerbates our identity crises is that many times, our experiences live up to our feelings and thoughts. I know I am saved and that I do sin, so it makes sense that I am a sinner saved by grace. The enemy of our souls uses the Big Three to carry out his spiritual overthrow. A defeated and frustrated believer makes a good advertisement for the kingdom of darkness as to why a person should stay away from Christianity.

Here is one indisputable fact: the devil has no defense against the truth. The word of God is truth. This is why Jesus (the Living Word) said, *"It is written"* and quoted the written word every time Satan tried to lure Him away from His identity or use His identity for personal gain (Luke 4:1–13, NKJV). The word of God was, is, and will always be the standard for truth. For us to live up to our callings and our new-creation identities, we must demand that our experiences rise to the level of truth. In other words, we must make sure that the Big Three, our thinking, our feelings, and our experiences, come into line with the word of God. Even though our thinking, our feelings, and our experiences are real, they may not be true, so we should never rely on them to be what determines truth is for us. If that were the case, we would have many standards for truth because not everyone thinks or feels the same way about everything. That would make truth relative. Truth would always be relative to someone's particular frame of reference, making absolute truth nonexistent. Truth is absolute because it is true at all times and in all places, no matter the circumstances. Absolute truth cannot be changed. Jesus said, "Sanctify them by Your truth. *Your word is truth"* (John 17:17, NKJV; emphasis added). Since the word of God is absolute truth, it must be the standard that our thoughts, feelings, and experiences are judged by. What the word of God said was true yesterday, it is still true today, and it will be true tomorrow. Truth is absolutely true.

No Middle Ground

Reality is whatever God says about something. It does not have to be proven; neither does it depend on circumstances. Anything that is in opposition to what God says is only imaginary. When God looks at something, He sees it as *either-or*; there are only two options. There is no middle ground with God. God is not into mixture. He never has been.

In the beginning, God set the *either-or* principle in place. He separated night from day and light from darkness. From Genesis to Revelation, you will find no middle ground. Let me give you a short list of *either-or*. Jesus said there are only two kinds of people: those who are with Him and those who are against Him. He said a person is either gathering or a person is scattering (Matthew 12:30, NKJV). There is no middle ground with God—no fence-sitters.

There are only two kingdoms: the kingdom of darkness and the kingdom of light (Colossians 1:13, NKJV). There are only two realms: the natural realm and the spiritual realm (1 Corinthians 2:14–16, NKJV). A person is either spiritually alive, or a person is spiritually dead (Ephesians 2:1–5, NKJV). A person is either saved or lost. A person is either obedient, or he or she is disobedient (Luke 19:10, NKJV). There is belief, and there is unbelief. Again, there is no in-between.

Here is the one I want to zero in on, because this is the one the deep-state actors will use in their attempts to overthrow our spiritual identities and to manipulate and control us. A person is either in the Spirit or the person is in the flesh. It is impossible to be in both. It is an *either-or*. Since it is impossible to be in the Spirit and in the flesh at the same time, can a child of God leave the Spirit and get in the flesh? The answer is an unequivocal no. How many times have you said or heard it said, "I got in the flesh?" What does this mean? It means we said or did something that was contrary to our new-creation natures. We acted like the people we used to be before we accepted and received Jesus as our Lord and Savior. The Big Three were involved: how we think, the way we feel, and what we do. It seems to validate the belief that I am a sinner saved by grace. I am saved and I do sin, so I must be a sinner saved by grace. Our experiences are certainly real, but the truth is that we are saints who acted in a way that is contrary to our new-creation natures.

Seed Will Bear after Its Own Kind

I think it would be a good idea to slow-walk our way through our spiritual identities. Let's begin with the seed. "The land produced vegetation—all sorts of seed-bearing plants, and trees with seed-bearing fruit. Their *seeds produced plants and trees of the same kind.* And God saw that it was good" (Genesis 1:12, NLT; emphasis added). We know that a seed will produce after its own kind, so we are not surprised to get cotton when we plant a cotton seed. What would be a surprise is if we were to get corn when we planted a cotton seed. A farmer can rest assured that the seed he or she planted will produce after its kind.

"Now Adam had sexual relations with his wife, Eve, and she became pregnant. When she gave birth to Cain, she said, 'With the Lord's help I have produced a man!' Later she gave birth to his brother and named him Abel" (Genesis 4:1–2, NLT). This took place after Adam and Eve had disobeyed God by eating from the forbidden tree. Because of their sin of disobedience and unbelief, God removed them from the garden of Eden. Sin had corrupted the seed of Adam, and he produced life after his kind. "And Adam lived one hundred and thirty years, and *begot a son in his own likeness, after is image* and named him Seth" (Genesis 5:3, NKJV; emphasis added). Again, we see Adam's seed producing after its kind.

Adam's willful disobedience affected the entire human race. "These wicked people are *born sinners;* even *from birth* they have lied and gone their own way" (Psalms 58:3, NLT; emphasis added). Adam's fall affected us all. His sinful seed was passed on to the entire human race. When we were physically born (born from below), we bore a sinful nature that we inherited from the first Adam. His sinful seed still bears after its kind. Paul described this state as being in the flesh (Romans 8:8, NKJV).

In 1 Corinthians, Paul talks about the first Adam and the last Adam. The first Adam became a living being. He received life. The last Adam became a life-giving spirit. He gives life (1 Corinthians

15:45, NKJV). The first Adam was disobedient to God's word. The last Adam was obedient to God's word. Both Adams bear seed after their kind. The first Adam's seed is sinful. The last Adam's seed is sinless. A person is either in the first Adam—bearing his seed—or the person is in the last Adam (Jesus) and bear His seed (Romans 5:17–20, NKJV). It is impossible to be in both at the same time or to be partially in one and partially in the other one. There is no middle ground. It is *either-or.*

This is why Jesus said that we must have a second birth date. To be born again actually means to be born from above (John 3:3, NKJV). Paul describes this state as being in the Spirit (Romans 8:9, NKJV). He says that we are either in the Spirit (saved) or we are in the flesh (lost), but we cannot be in both.

To be born from below is to be born into the natural realm by the natural birth process, and it is through the sinful seed of the first Adam. At our physical births, we bear the nature of the first Adam. To be born from above is to be born into the spiritual realm, and it is through the sinless seed of the last Adam. We bear the nature of the last Adam (Jesus Christ) now that we have been born again. To be born from below is to be in the flesh (Romans 8:8, NKJV). To be born from above is to be in the Spirit (Romans 8:9, NKJV). There is no in-between. We cannot be in both places at the same time.

Is it possible for us as believers to leave the Spirit and reenter the flesh, and then move back into the Spirit? No, it is not; but that is exactly what would have to happen if we were sinners saved by grace. We would have to leave our new-creation identities (the Spirit), reenter our old identities (the flesh), and then return to our new-creation identities.

Let's keep this slow-walk thought process going for a moment. Is it possible for someone who is not born again to leave the flesh, enter the Spirit, do good works, and then return to the flesh? The question is not, can a lost person do good works? He or she certainly can, and the person may get credit for it here on earth, but the individual will not be rewarded for it in heaven. The question is, can a person who has never had a second birth date leave his or her flesh nature, enter the Spirit, and perform good works? The answer is an overwhelming *no*! No is the correct answer. Yet, we have been convinced that we can leave the Spirit, reenter our old lives that were crucified and buried, do bad stuff, and then reenter the Spirit. This is what we believe when we say that we are sinners saved by grace.

It is spiritually impossible to move back and forth from the flesh to the Spirit, or from the Spirit to the flesh. I have not met a spiritual Houdini yet. Now, it is possible set our minds on the flesh, and if this is our choice, then we will find ourselves living by the flesh. But that is not the same thing as being in the flesh. It is living life apart from our true identities, and there can be grave consequences when we choose to do so.

Is it possible for us as new-creation beings to do bad things? Yes, it is. Doesn't that prove that we are sinners saved by grace? No, it does not. Paul's letter to the Christians who were living in Rome answers this question very succinctly. If we set our minds on the flesh, we will live according to the flesh (Romans 8:5–17, NKJV). Once again, setting our minds on the flesh and living by the flesh are not the same thing as reentering the flesh. When we do things that do not jibe with our new-creation identities, we are acting in a way that is not true to our new natures as children of God. Those bad choices do come with consequences.

The Lord is holy, and He cannot and will not cohabit with sin. All through the New Testament, we read about Christ being in us and us being in Christ. There are more references about us being in Christ. As God's children, we have more than a relationship with Christ; we are in union with Him. We are partakers of His divine nature (2 Peter 1:4, NKJV). As He is, so are we in this world (1 John 4:17, NKJV). Think about this: If we have two natures, a sinful one and a sinless one, in essence, we are saying that God will do what He says He will not do, and that is to cohabit with sin. If what we think, feel, and experience is not in line with the word of God, what needs to change? The word of God is absolute truth, so it will never change. That leaves us with one option—the Big Three. What we think, the way we feel, and our experiences must be brought into line with the word of God.

In writing to the church in Corinth, Paul says, "Don't you realize that your body is the temple of the Holy Spirit, who lives in you and was given to you by God" (1 Corinthians 6:19, NLT). If we still had our old natures, God could not live in us because He will not cohabit with sin. Our old natures were sinful because it came from the contaminated seed of the first Adam. Here is a great quote from Clark Whitten's book, *Pure Grace*: "God will not live in a dirty house."

Jesus Was Made What I Was so I Could Be What He Is

As new creations in Christ, are we literally righteous, or are we positionally righteous? When we accepted Jesus's invitation to life, was righteousness imputed to us, or was righteousness imparted to us? Getting the answer to this question right is a game changer. Let me ask this question in another way. Were we made righteous the moment we were saved, or did God deposit righteousness into our heavenly identity bank account for a future withdrawal?

To human reasoning, being positionally righteous makes sense because it is in lock-step with the way we think, feel, and act at times. And since it makes sense, being positionally righteous must be the correct answer. Right? Wrong! The deep-state actors within us love it when we allow our everchanging thoughts, feelings, and experiences to determine what is true and not true. When we allow the Big Three to manipulate and control us, we will always live beneath our callings (Ephesians 4:1, NKJV).

Before we accepted and received Jesus Christ as our Lord and Savior, we were sinners. This is indisputable. Here's the question that needs to be answered. Were we literal sinners, or were we positional sinners? In all the years I've been in the ministry, I have never met a person who has said that we were positional sinners. Why? Because of our experiences. Our experiences align with the word of God.

The word of God says that we were sinners. Our experiences say, "Yes, we were." The sinful nature of the first Adam was not imputed (accredited) to us; his sinful nature was imparted to us.

"For as by one man's [the first Adam] disobedience many were made sinners, so also by one Man's [Jesus—the last Adam] obedience many will be made righteous" (Romans 5:19, NKJV; emphasis added). Again, we have an *either-or* in this verse. We are *either* in the first Adam (our old natures) *or* we are in Jesus the last Adam (our new natures), but we cannot be in both. There is no going back and forth from one to the other. "For He [God] made Him [Jesus] who knew no sin to be sin for us, that we might become the righteousness of God in Him" (2 Corinthians 5:21, NKJV; emphasis added). Jesus was made what I was so I could be what He is.

If it were possible for us to move from the Spirit back into the flesh, then back into the Spirit, Christ would be cohabiting with sin, since "Christ is in us" and "we are in Christ." The old nature is sinful. There is nothing good in the old nature. Paul tells us that the old man (nature) was crucified with Christ and the body of sin was done away with (Romans 6:6, NKJV). The body of sin is referring to the old nature. The old man (nature) was the evidence that was against us; it proved without a shadow of doubt that we were sinners. The old man (nature) was crucified and buried. The old nature no longer exists. It is impossible to enter something that does not exist. Our battle is with the flesh, not with the old nature. When we waste precious time and energy fighting something that does not exist, it is easy to become the devil's personal chattel.

How God sees us and what God says about us is what determines our spiritual identities. Remember, whatever God says is reality. Our identities are not determined by what we think, how we feel, or by our experiences, even when it makes sense to our human reasoning. "For the eyes of the Lord are on the righteous, and His ears are open to their prayers; but the face of the Lord is against those who do evil" (1 Peter 3:12, NKJV). The Lord sees us as being righteous. He is not looking at us through a spiritual filter. He sees us as new creations. The old versions of us no longer exist. "Little children, let no one deceive you. He who practices righteousness is righteous *just as He is righteous*" (1 John 3:7, NKJV; emphasis added).

The life of Christ, His death, and His resurrection eviscerated the enemy's ability to do anything to God's children without their permission. He has absolutely no defense against the truth. This is why Jesus told us, "If you abide in My word, you are My disciples indeed, and you shall know the truth, and the truth shall make you free" (John 8:31–32, NKJV). When we make our home in the word of God, we will know the truth, and the truth we know will not only set us free; the truth we know will keep us free. What we need to do is spend less time on Facebook and more time in the Faith Book.

As new-creation beings, we will sin, but that does not make us sinners saved by grace. We are not sinners by nature. We are saints who sometimes make poor choices. When we get a deeper and broader understanding of our new-creation identities, we will not be sinless, but we will certainly sin less.

If we only knew … We should now.

Conclusion

"What you don't know won't hurt you." That may be a nifty little quote, and it may even be true in some cases, but when it comes to living a victorious life of faith, ignorance may not be bliss after all. God's people are still being destroyed for a lack of knowledge, especially when it comes to our identities as children of God. Most of the family of God is not living up to who they are in Christ or enjoying their birthright privileges. Most do not even know what their family privileges are. The words that Jesus spoke to the Samaritan woman during their well-side chat are still ringing through the corridors of time: "If you only knew the Gift of God" (John 4:10, NKJV).

What we have in Christ was not gained through human achievement. No one is good enough or can do enough for long enough to be declared righteous before God. As children of God, we do not have what we have because of our good works. We have what we have despite our works. Right standing before God is not secured by personal accomplishments. We did not earn our birthrights. As children of God, our birthright privileges come from divine accomplishment. Jesus Christ did for us what we could not do for ourselves. He was good enough, and He did enough for all of us, who will accept and receive Him as our Lord and Savior. It is all about His worth, not our works. He gets all the glory!

God is pleased with our good works, but we are not accepted by Him because of our good works. This is why it is called grace. What we need to do is accept it, believe it, and conform our lives to

179

it. "Yes, everything else is worthless when compared with the infinite value of knowing Christ Jesus my Lord. For his sake I have discarded everything else, counting it all as garbage, so that I could gain Christ and become one with him. *I no longer count on my own righteousness through_obeying the law*; rather, *I become righteous through faith in Christ*. For God's way of making us right with himself depends on faith" (Philippians 3:8, NLT; emphasis added). Again, it is all about His worth, not about our works.

Profoundly Simple, Yet Simply Profound

There is a principle that has the power to dramatically impact your life. This principle is profoundly simple, yet simply profound. There is a small price that has to be paid. Are you ready for it? You will have to die. This makes the principle difficult, because there is nothing as strong as self-preservation. But, if we are willing to pay the price, then we can really start living.

I am not talking about dying physically. I am talking about dying to self, giving up what we want for what God wants. When what God wants becomes more important to us than what we want, we are dying to ourselves. We are now in position to live the abundant life that Jesus came to give. This is what Paul was talking about when he said, "My old self has been crucified with Christ. It is no longer I who lives but Christ lives in me. So I live in this earthly body by trusting in the Son of God, who loved me and gave himself for me" (Galatians 2:20, NLT). That sounds simple enough, but you may find it to be one of the most difficult things you will ever do. Paul is not speaking metaphorically when he talks about Christ living His life in and through us. The word of God confirms the fact that Jesus Christ literally and practically dwells within every believer. Christ is not living on the outside of us just to be our helper in our time of need. He has made His home within us and is with us all the time. "So you also should consider yourselves to be dead to the power of sin and alive to God through Christ Jesus" (Romans 6:11, NLT).

We Are Earthen Vessels

Paul describes a believer as an earthen vessel that has content, "For it is the God who commanded light to shine out of darkness, who has shone in our hearts to give the light of the knowledge of the glory of God in the face of Jesus Christ. But we have this treasure [Jesus Christ] in earthen vessels [bodies], that the excellence of the power may be of God and not of us" (2 Corinthians 4:6–7, NKJV; emphasis added). Christ is the treasure that lives in every believer, and His purpose is to reveal the glory of God through us.

It is a shame that dying is the last thing we do, because it can teach us so much about living. *If we only knew the gift of God.*

Chapter Briefs

CHAPTER 1

I have found that a large percentage of Christians are pretty confident they are going to heaven someday, but they are not having a heavenly time getting there. They remind me of an old iron bedstead that is firm on both ends, but it sags in the middle. On one end, they know they are saved. On the other end, they know they are going to heaven, but life sags in between the two ends.

God so loved the world that He gave His best gift, His Son, Jesus Christ. A gift is a wrapped container that has content. It is possible to accept a gift but never open it to receive its contents. God's present (Jesus) brought His presence (Holy Spirit) to the earth realm. Jesus is not only God's present to you; He is God's presence in you. Along with His presence are all the birthright privileges that come with being His child.

Jesus is the wrapped container. He is God's gift to you. In Him is not only life, but a life that is abundant. Jesus overflows with content. When we accept Jesus (God's gift to the world) as our Lord and Savior, we not only get Him; we get everything that is in Him as well. There is more, so much more, in Jesus than just forgiveness of sins. That in and of itself would be worth accepting the gift. Jesus said that He came to give us life, a life that is full and abundant.

Chapter 2

Being more than a conqueror has nothing to do with human prowess, intellectual acumen, or being tough; it is about not allowing situations or circumstances, no matter how difficult they may be, to rob us of the peace and security that we have in Christ. We survive every storm by placing our confidence in the anchor (Jesus), who is more than able to steady our souls in the midst of all storms.

To live like a victor and not a victim, we must have the mentality of a conqueror. Our thinking must be brought in to line with our new-creation identities. When we accepted Christ's invitation to life and received Him as our Lord and Savior, there was an exchange of identity. Our old identities were exchanged for new ones; our old natures for a new nature. We were given eternal life. Something that is eternal has no beginning. If it had a beginning, it could not be eternal. Since God is eternal, He has no beginning. Since our new natures are eternal, our new natures have no beginning. Therefore, our new-creation identities have no past. The enemy loves to throw the past in our faces to keep us from seeing who we are in Christ. When we know and are confident in our identities as a child of God, we will not allow the enemy of our souls to use something that does not exist to defeat us.

Our God is bigger than any circumstance or situation that we may find ourselves in. A more-than-a-conqueror does not tell God how big his or her problems are; a more-than-a-conqueror tells their problems how big their God is.

Chapter 3

It is hard to live like a child of God when we have a slave's mentality. Just because we are children of God by our spiritual births does not mean we live mistake-free lives. Sometimes we make bad decisions and do things that violate our new-creation natures. How can God love us when we willfully disobey? What does He think about us when we mess up? The parable that Jesus told about a father and his two sons should answer that question for us.

Even though the youngest son had made poor choices, his father received him unconditionally when he returned home. He was not put on probation, lectured, or confined to his room for a period of time. He was completely restored. Why? Because he was his father's son. The only way the father could treat him was like a son, even though the son was thinking like a slave.

There is one very important element to this story that is so easy to overlook. It is incredibly liberating too. The younger son did waste his livelihood on riotous living, but he did not lose his inheritance. Our heavenly Father is not out for revenge when we choose to live like servants; He is always ready to restore us when we come to our senses.

CHAPTER 4

No matter how often you try to quench the thirst of your soul with the things of this world, you will always be left empty. The wells of this world are not deep enough and the water is not pure enough to satisfy the craving of the human soul. The return trip to draw more water will never end because spiritual thirst cannot be satisfied by physical things.

The Samaritan woman was living with a man who was not her husband. She was not going to risk another failed marriage and all the pain that comes with it. She had five failed marriages before she was in this live-in relationship. That says a lot about what her empty soul was crying out for. She just wanted someone to love her unconditionally and to be her covenant partner. What she was looking for was sitting on the well-curb that day, waiting for her to come to draw water. She was going to find in the seventh man what she had been searching for her entire life.

The Samaritan woman thought her problem was that she could not find the right soul mate. What she thought was her problem, was not her actual problem, and that was her problem. She was looking for love in all the wrong places. She and her water pot had something in common. They were both empty. Little did she know that what she was searching for would be found in the man who is the living water and who was sitting on the curb of the well. His name is Jesus.

Chapter 5

Faith is not about everything turning out all right. Faith is about being all right no matter how things turn out. It does not matter how difficult or challenging our circumstances may be, with Christ, we not only have the strength to persevere, but we can persist with a good attitude.

Our attitudes will always be decided by where we choose to place our faith. Where we focus our faith will determine our positions and where we choose to stand. Our positions will determine our perspectives and how we see things. How we see things will be decided by who or what we place our confidence in.

When times of trouble and testing come, we have a choice. We can keep them in our faces and be overpowered by them, or we can put them in God's face. If our choices are to keep them in our own faces, we may find ourselves as victims. By choosing to put them in God's face, we are able to see things differently because we are able to see them from a new position. Our new position gives us a new perspective. We discover that, with Christ, all things are Him-possible.

It is our attitude, not our aptitude, that determines our altitude. How high we fly in this life will be determined by our attitudes, not by how smart we are. With Christ, all things are Him-possible.

Chapter 6

There is one thing that hurting people share aside from their wounds. Hurt people have the propensity to hurt people. There is no way for anyone to go through life without being wounded. It would be easier to climb a thorn tree without any clothes on and with a wildcat under each arm and not get a scratch, than it would be to go through life and not get wounded. Getting hurt and feeling pain is a part of living life.

Many adults are carrying and nurturing wounds they received during their childhoods. In order to protect themselves from future hurts and pain, they have a tendency to make inner vows, such as, "No one will ever hurt me again." "I will never trust another human being as long as I live." "I will never let anyone get close to me again." To make an inner vow is to tell God that you will take charge of certain areas of your life. That is a recipe for failure and a setup for more hurt. Hurt people who continually pick at their wounds will smell like what they are going through or have been through.

As children of God, we are not exempt from pain. We never know when we are going to find ourselves in times of testing. But there is one thing we can count on: Jesus will always be with us, no matter what. We can come through any furnace experience and not smell like what we have been through.

CHAPTER 7

Peter was able to walk on the very thing that was threatening his life. The storm that was in his face was now under his feet. With the Lord's help, we can walk on what others sink in. If we keep our eyes on Jesus, we can walk on the things that keep us emotionally upset. There is one thing for certain: we will never walk on water if we stay inside the boat.

Storms are distractions. The enemy of our souls will use the storms we find ourselves in to get us to take our eyes off of Jesus. The Lord will use storms as an attraction to get us to fix our eyes on Him. There are times when we find ourselves in a situation like the trapeze artist; we feel like we are suspended in midair, between faith and fear. When that happens, what do we do? We must wait. During those waiting moments, remind yourself that there is only one catcher, and it is not you. You are the flier. The flier does nothing but let go. The catcher does everything else. The recipe for sinking in our storms is trying to catch the catcher. We must trust the catcher. "Be still and know that I am God" (Psalms 46:10, NKJV).

What we choose to focus on will influence what we are able to do. When Peter purposely focused his eyes on Jesus, he walked by faith on the very thing that was threatening his security—the storm. When his focus shifted from Jesus to his situation, he walked in fear and sank into the water.

Chapter 8

When it comes to living life, there are no do-overs. It is impossible for us to travel back in time and rewrite our histories. What has been done is done. But there is one thing that we can do: we can start where we are in our dashes (lives) and change the endings. We can finish the dashes between our birth dates and our death dates filled with intentional purpose. It is one thing to be alive; it is another thing to live. It is time we start living because our dashes are short.

I am afraid most of us have been convinced that it is impossible to live peaceful lives. Living in peace has nothing to do with not having stressful situations to deal with. Even in the difficult circumstances that we may find ourselves in, it is possible to remain in peace if we understand that our peace is found in Christ. He is our peace (Ephesians 2:14, NKJV).

"'I know the plans I have for you,' says the Lord. 'They are plans for good and not for disaster, *to give you a future and a hope*'" (Jeremiah 29:11, NKJV; italics added). God already knows the plan He has for you, and it is a good plan, too, a plan that is filled with hope. All you have to do is trust Him.

Since we are in this world, we will face difficult times. What we have to remember is that we are not of this world. If we choose to set our affections on things of this world, thinking they will bring us the peace and happiness that we are looking for, we will be sadly disappointed. A future with hope is what God has in mind for His children.

CHAPTER 9

If there is anything we need to know about temptation, it is these two things: temptation in and of itself is not sin, and God will never tempt you in order to test you.

Being victorious over temptation has nothing to do with our personal resolve or how strong we are mentally. This is not our way of escape. Jesus set the example for us on how to escape temptation. He demonstrated for us the way of escape. Our strength and escape route is in the word of God. Every time the devil would present a temptation, Jesus would say, "It is written." Jesus was the Living Word of God, and He took His stand on the written word of God. The more of the written word we have in us, the more His strength will flow through us.

The written word of God is the devil's kryptonite. He has no defense against the word of God. The devil is a liar, and he cannot stand in the presence of truth. When he speaks, he speaks lies. He is a liar and the father of all lies. God's word is truth, and truth exposes the devil's lies, which becomes our way of escape every time temptation comes knocking.

Being tempted is not a sin; neither does it mean that we are bad people when we are tempted. Jesus was tempted at all points as we are, yet He did not sin. Because He won, we win when we allow the word of God to be our way of escape.

CHAPTER 10

The battle we fight every day takes place between our ears. What consumes our minds will ultimately control our lives. This is why it is so important for us to take control of our thought lives.

"Plant a thought reap an action. Plant an action reap a habit. Plant a habit reap a character. Plant a character reap a destiny" (Ralph Waldo Emerson). The fruits of our thoughts are words. Words paint pictures that can lead to actions. Actions that are repeated can become habits.

Habits mold and shape character. Character then determines destiny. Having a good, healthy thought life is crucial to having a happy life. We are today what we thought yesterday. We will be tomorrow what we think about today.

There will be times when we will have unhealthy thoughts. When this happens, it does not mean that we are bad people. The enemy is faithful to his job description, and he will do everything he possible can to smuggle unhealthy thoughts into our heads. But we have the power to decide how long they stick around. We may not be able to keep bad thoughts from sneaking in occasionally, but we have maximum control over how long they stay. We need to evict them quickly.

CHAPTER 11

The purpose of a covenant is how God relates to humanity. Under the old covenant, God was not approachable, accessible, or available to the ordinary person. The Incarnation changed everything. God literally wrapped Himself up in human flesh and birthed Himself. His birthplace was a low-rise manger, not a high-rise mansion somewhere. This made Him approachable to anyone, no matter his or her rank in society. The up-and-out, as well as the down-and-out and all those in-between, have a standing invitation to approach Him.

Our birthright privileges as His children give us permission not only to come into His presence, but we can come with confidence and no fear. "So let us come boldly to the throne of our gracious God. There we will receive His mercy, and we will find grace to help when we need it most" (Hebrews 4:16, NLT).

The Psalmist said that God is our very present help (Psalms 46:10, NKJV). *Very present*, means that He is available at all times. Jesus never turned anyone away. Some of His prayer times were interrupted by people who came to seek His help. He always made Himself available. God is not a distant deity. He is our Abba, our Father, and He is always willing to spend time with you.

God is available for you. God is approachable by you. God is accessible to you.

CHAPTER 12

We will never have what we have not released. It can be our businesses, a child or our children, spouses, grandkids, marriages, relationships, our lives, or whatever. Releasing is difficult because it involves trust. God is trustworthy, but God cannot trust us with what we have not released. A miracle can happen only when we release whatever we are holding on to.

The stick that Moses held in his hand did not turn into a snake until he obeyed God and released it. The stick became the rod of God, and it was placed back into the hands of Moses. Jochebed, the mother of Moses, did not see a miracle until she took her hands off of the basket that her baby boy lay in, and released it into the reeds of the river. She was allowed to raise her own child in the home of Pharaoh and received wages for doing so.

Here is the beautiful thing about releasing. Once we release whatever we are holding on to, God will perform a miracle and then place it back into our hands to be used for His glory. We really never have what we refuse to turn loose. What we refuse to release will ultimately have us.

The reason it is so hard to turn loose of things comes from a lack of trust on our part. Can God be trusted? Always remember this, whatever God is, He is completely. Since He is trustworthy, He is completely trustworthy.

CHAPTER 13

When we have a giant showdown moment, our positions will be one of fear or one of faith. Both fear and faith believe something is going to happen. One is bad, and one is good. The men of Israel were full of fear because they were looking at Goliath. He was too big, and they felt there was no way they could take on Goliath. What they were looking at exposed their weaknesses.

David was full of faith because he was looking at God. His God was too big to fail, and he believed he could take out Goliath. What David was looking at revealed his strength. How David and the men of Israel saw things determined what they believed. What they believed determined what they were able to do.

The same is true with us when we are facing life challenges. It is not *if* we face giants, it is *when*. Giants come in all shapes and sizes. Our giants can be financial, health issues, marriages, relationships, businesses, or anything that appears to be overwhelming. How we perform when that happens will be determined by our perspectives; our perspectives will be determined by the positions we choose to look at our giants from. It will be a position of fear or a position of faith.

David was unmoved by the overwhelming odds he was facing in the natural realm. He knew his resources came from the spiritual realm, so he drew his strength from God. The position David chose allowed him to have a perspective that empowered his performance. He took the giant out.

Chapter 14

If we could write an epitaph for the story of the father and his two boys that was told by Jesus in Luke 15, it might read something like this: "Our heavenly Father will accept sinners unconditionally and love them extravagantly."

It is possible to know all about the Father and not to know the Father. This is the motivation behind Jesus telling this story. How does the Father see us, and how does He feel about us? This story is about the father.

When the father saw his youngest son returning home, he ran to him. No lecture was given; no probation period was levied; the son was embraced, loved on, and welcomed home. When the father saw his eldest son returning from the field and he refused to come inside and join the party, the father went out to him. No lecture was given. The father lovingly reminded the eldest son of his birthright privileges and that celebrating the return of his brother was the right thing to do.

We spend a lot of time talking about the two boys in this parable, when the spotlight should actually be on the father. His love for both of his sons never wavered. The elder son was given the same thing that his younger brother received, and he did not realize it. He was given grace. The father extended grace to both of them. They were his sons, and that is the only way the father could treat them.

It is possible for us to share our Father's home but not share His heart.

Chapter 15

Life is filled with moments when we feel the squeeze of a test. When that happens, we need to remember what James wrote in chapter 1 of his epistle. We are not the object of the test; our faith is—trials are cleansing moments that will flush out the toxins that have secretly invaded our lives. There will be those moments when we get to see if we are just talk, or if we really believe what we say we believe.

James uses the word *various* in describing trials. We get our English word *polka dot* from this word. That is an interesting choice of words. Trials are like polka dots; they come in all colors and sizes. Life has its testing times, and when they come, James says that we can face them with a mindset of joy. That is only possible if we know who we are in Christ and what is going on when difficult times hit.

When you find yourself in the middle of a furnace moment, it does not mean you have done something wrong. You can do the right thing and life can fall apart on you. You can pull the right levers, push the right buttons, and things can blow up in your face. Life can be unfair. As long as we are in this life, we will have trials and times of testing, and it is not because God is unfair or is not good. All the unfairness and evil in the world that affects every person, both the good and the bad, is man's fault, not God's. God is good, and whatever God is, He is completely. He is completely good.

CHAPTER 16

Events in life can leave us devastated at times, but as long as we have an ear to hear and a leg to stand on, it is not over. We can keep living even when everything in us is screaming to quit. Thomas Edison was spot on when he said, "The most certain way to succeed is always to try just one more time." Quitting is always an option, but not for a winner.

We have a proclivity to judge what will happen tomorrow based on what happens today. If our hope is determined by the good or the bad that we experience during any given day, we will be jerked around like a kite on a string in a high wind, sailing along nicely one moment, and then nose-diving the next. This is why it is so important to place our focus on Jesus, because He is the author and finisher of our faith.

Hope, or the lack of it, is determined by what we choose to focus our attention on. It is a choice. We can look at how big our problems are, or we can focus on how big our God is. There is only one way out of hopelessness, and that way is Jesus. Jesus said that He is the door, the gate, and the way. A door makes it possible for us to enter or egress something. Jesus is our way of escaping hopelessness, and He is our entrance into hope. He is the only one who has the power to take "lessness" out of hope. As our door, He makes it possible for us to escape the enemy of despair and enter His joy.

CHAPTER 17

Jesus Christ lives His life through dead people. When we accepted Christ and received Him as our Lord and Savior, He came to live in the deepest parts of our inner-most beings, our spirits. We now have new lives in Christ, and He is the source of our new lives. Christ not only lives in us; He wants to express Himself through us. He does this through our souls, which are our thoughts, our feelings, and our will—what we do. Christ is our life.

Our heart is Christ's home, and He wants to have full run of the house. When we realize that we are dead and that Christ is living His life through us as us, we will be strong no matter what life throws at us. The victorious Christian life is not about doing all you can, the best you can, for as long as you can; it is realizing that you can't, but He can.

When we had our born-from-above experiences with Christ, we did not just receive new lives; we received Christ, who is our life. Our tendency is to separate the things of God from God. When we accepted Christ as our way, we accepted Him because He is our way, not something distinct from Him. When we accepted Him as our life, we got Him because He is our life.

Christ has not only given us a new life; He is our life—Christ in you, you in Christ. "We have become partakers of His divine nature" (2 Peter 1:4, NKJV).

CHAPTER 18

Ignorance is not knowing something, but not wanting to know is something else. It is one thing to not know who you are as a child of God; it is another thing to not want to know who you are as a child of God. Ignorance can have a lot of negative consequences, but lacking common sense can be devastating. Both are a choice.

The enemy of our souls knows that he cannot undo what God has done in our lives, but he also knows that if he can keep us in the dark as to what God has done in our lives, we will never live up to our identities as new creations.

Here is some good news: There is an awakening within the body of Christ about what happened to a person when he or she had his or her born-from-above experience. The Holy Spirit is bringing an incredible revelation about a believer's identity to those who are hungry to know. God does fill the hearts of the hungry with good things (Luke 1:53, NKJV). We need to pay attention. It is a matter of remaining ignorant or choosing to know the truth. Truth that we know is what sets us free, and truth keeps us free.

What stunts our spiritual growth more than anything, is thinking spiritual maturity is about information, when it is really about transformation. Our heads can grow from being full of knowledge, while our spirits remain dwarfed from malnourishment.

Since we have been given free will, it becomes our decision about on how long we are without knowledge concerning our identities as children of God. Ignorance may be bliss in some areas, but certainly not when it comes to knowing who we are in Christ. We can know our identities if we want to know. It is a question of, does our want-to want to?

Chapter 19

There is absolutely nothing that is in our pasts, in our presents, or in our futures that God does not know. God is omniscient, which means there is nothing He does not know. If it were possible for us to do something that God did not know we would do, then we could disappoint Him. Since that will never happen, we can never disappoint God. Ever.

Since God knows the future before it happens, Adam and Eve's disobedience did not surprise Him. Since God knew what they would do, He was not disappointed when they did it. The only way He could have been disappointed with them was if they had done something that He did not know they would do. Since God cannot be surprised or caught off guard, He cannot be disappointed.

God does not think the way we think. He just knows. God does not go through a thinking process to form an opinion about anything. He already has His opinion. What He thinks is the way it is, too. God does not have to bring His thoughts in line with our thoughts. We must bring our thoughts in line with His.

Since God possesses full knowledge about everything, His thoughts never change. Our thinking is always being aligned with reality. God's thoughts are reality. "Let this mind be in you, which was also in Christ Jesus" (Philippians 2:5, NKJV).

CHAPTER 20

It was not humanity's goodness that attracted God; it was His love for humanity, even when humanity did not want anything to do with Him. There was nothing in us that attracted God. It was His love for us that drew Him.

Good works will never be the reason anyone is ever declared righteous before God. Our justifications, our legal standings before God, will never be because God saw so much good in us that He just had to accept us. We were not worthy to be saved, but God saw that we were worth saving. If we are worth saving, then we are worth providing for.

God is the only one who can take what is unworthy and make it worthy. He can take what is unfit and make it fit. When we come to the Lord, in essence, we are saying, "Lord, there is nothing in me that is deserving of your love and acceptance. You are my only hope. There is nothing in me that is deserving of your presence. I am coming to you because I am unworthy." It is our unworthiness that makes God approachable. Our goodness is not what attracts the Lord. It is His love for us, therefore; He deserves all the glory.

Our happiness in life depends on how we think God sees and feels about us. If we have an unhealthy opinion about how God feels about us, it will affect our abilities to live successful lives of faith. How can you trust someone when you are not sure if they really love you or not? When we see ourselves the way God sees us, it can change our entire perspective on life. It is important for us to know that we are children of God and that He is madly in love with us.

CHAPTER 21

Most Christians are ignorant of the very thing that God does not want us to be ignorant about. "I don't want you *to be ignorant* brethren, *concerning those who have fallen asleep,* lest you sorrow as others who have no hope" (1 Thessalonians 4:13, NKJV; emphasis added). Paul uses the expression *falling asleep* in this verse to describe death for a child of God. There is nothing dreadful or fearful in falling asleep.

Paul also addresses the subject of grieving over the death of a loved one in this passage. He does not say a believer should never grieve when a loved one dies. That would not be a fair expectation. When you love someone, you will grieve when death separates you. Grieving is the price for loving. A child of God has hope so he or she does not grieve like those who have no hope. Our hope comes from knowing that Christ's death took life out of death for us. For us, death has no sting, and the grave has no victory. Death is dead to a believer. When you accepted God's gift of life and received Jesus as your Lord and Savior, death lost its claim on you. For you, death is only the vehicle that carries you into God's presence.

Paul ends his short teaching on death for a child of God and the return of Christ with these words: "Therefore *comfort* one another with these words" (1 Thessalonians 4:18, NKJV; emphasis added). The word *comfort* means to strengthen, to fortify, to make strong, to give courage. It is comforting to know that death is not the end for a child of God; it is actually the beginning.

Chapter 22

Even though our thoughts, feelings, and experiences can be spot on at times, because they are ever-changing, we should never depend on them to define what is true or not true for us. The unchangeable word of God should be our standard for truth. God's word has always been true, and it will always be true. Our thoughts, feelings, and experiences should be brought into line with the word of God, not the other way around.

How God sees us and what God thinks about us is what determines our spiritual identities. Whatever God says is reality. Our identities are not determined by what we think, how we feel, or by our experiences;

even when it makes sense to our human reasoning. The Lord sees us as righteous: "For the eyes of the Lord are on the righteous" (1 Peter 3:12, NKJV). God is not looking at us through some spiritual filter. He sees us as new creations.

When we accepted and received Jesus Christ as our Lord and Savior, righteousness was imparted to us. We were made righteous (2 Corinthians 5:21, NKJV). As new creations in Christ, we are not positionally righteous any more than we were positionally sinners before we were born again. As new-creation beings, we bear the nature of the sinless seed of Jesus Christ, who is called the last Adam (2 Corinthians 5:17, NKJV). As a child of God, you bear His nature (2 Peter 1:4, NKJV). You are literally righteous, and since you did not do anything to be made righteous, you cannot do anything to become unrighteous. You cannot lose with your bad works what you did not get with you good works. As He (Jesus) is, so are you in this world (1 John 4:17, NKJV).

Printed in the United States
by Baker & Taylor Publisher Services